PAGES FROM THE BOOK OF THE SUN
NEW AND SELECTED POEMS

NIYI OSUNDARE

Africa World Press, Inc.

P.O. Box 1892
Trenton, NJ 08607

P.O. Box 48
Asmara, ERITREA

Africa World Press, Inc.

P.O. Box 1892
Trenton, NJ 08607

P.O. Box 48
Asmara, ERITREA

Cover Artwork: untitled by Moyo Ogundipe
Cover Design: Ashraful Haque
Book Design: Krystal Jackson and Roger Dormann

Library of Congress Cataloging-in-Publication Data

Osundare, Niyi, 1947-
    Pages from the book of the sun : new and selected poems / Niyi Osundare
        p. cm.
    ISBN 0-86543-867-6 -- ISBN 0-86543-868-4 (pbk.)
    1. Nigeria--Poetry. I. Title.

PR9387.9.O866 P34 2000
821'.914--dc21

00-033217

Contents

New Poems

PEOPLE ARE MY CLOTHES

Cheerful drumming, with gangan (talking drum) in the lead, then the song:

Ènìà lasoo mi
Ènìà lasoo mi
Tí mo bá bojú wèhìn tí mo rénii mi
Ènìà lasoo mi...[1]

People are my clothes
People are my clothes
When I look right, when I look left
When I look back and see my folk

My head swells like a jubilant mountain
My heart leaps in infinite joy

> People are my clothes
> My raiment dwells the loom of teeming folds

I am the alligator pepper seed
With siblings too many for the numbering eye
I am a seminal drop in the bowl of the sea,
A thread in the loom of the sky

> People are my clothes
> My raiment dwells the loom of teeming folds

Let people be my robe
> As the savannah grass secures the deer

Let people be my robe
> As the plumage surrounds the bird

Not for me the porcupine
  Which peeps at the world
  From a bunker of thorns

Not for me the tortoise
  Whose carapace sharpens
  A sword around its neck

    People are my clothes
    My raiment   dwells the loom of teeming folds

One morsel can never make a feast
One finger cannot retrieve a fallen needle
One leg cannot win a race
One broomstick cannot sweep the marketplace

A lone hyena will come to grief
In a flock of resolute sheep
A lone tree cannot stand the fury
Of the desert storm
The masquerade who strays
Too far from its followers
Soon loses its mask in a rude, unholy lane

With many steps the foot will tame
The tyranny of the road
With all the fingers the hand
Will grab the mightiest machete
From that machete
Let twilight come to the tree of pain

    People are my clothes
    My raiment dwells the loom of teeming folds

People are my clothes
People are my clothes

My billowy brocade, my sumptuous silk
My loom is the thronging street
Busy workbenches, farmlands of fruiting trees;
Its shuttle is the care-ful word,
Which runs life's thread from coast to coast.
A song swells in my throat,
Awaiting the chorus of a waking world

People are my clothes
My raiment dwells the loom of teeming folds

People are my clothes
People are my clothes
When I look right, when I look left
When I look back and see my folk
My heart leaps with infinite joy
People are my clothes
I will never fear the rage of chilling storms

People are my clothes
My raiment dwells the loom of teeming folds

Enia lasoo mi
Bi mo ba boju wehin ti mo renii mi
Enia lasoo mi...

1. The first stanza carries a translation of this song

TELLING GIFT
(for Roxy Akayejo)

You have given a pen to a poet
And thrown open the door to the house of songs

With this pen I will plumb the depth
Of seen things, of things unseen
Till fallow pages, drill little lights
Through the quarry of silent stones

Amaze the sun with secrets
Of the night below its feet
Stir sleeping moons, quicken buried stars
Tickle dark tunnels with the fire of its nib

I will dye the season's robes
In the indigo of its ink
Surprise white surfaces with a blackness
Dense with song and sense

The pen in my hand is a long-sought assegai[1]
Tipped with vinegar and honey
Feathered by wisdom

This pen knows the dust of rooted spaces
Of breaking waters and cradles purple with
memory
Crimsom tales of the sundering,
Of distances and seamless oceans

This pen knows the song of scars
Sorrow boulevards in happy kingdoms
The soundless detonation of dreams long deferred
Moatless chasms of the castle of our skin

This pen breaks bread with beggars
On the streets of the sun
Stirs little storms in the stomachs of eating chiefs
Confronts the emperor with the monster in the mrror

This pen will soar like an eagle
Dive like a dolphin
Join earthworms in their dialogue with the earth
Give Memory a mask, then a meaning.

You have given a pen to a poet
And thrown open the door to the house of songs

1. Spear

THRESHOLDS
(Millennium song)

Feet washed by a thousand rains
We passage through the season's threshold;
Steps creak under our soles, quick with questions,
Curious with the tangled map of new crossings...

Crossings
Millennial shells cracking into moons
Traversing skyface with a caravan of riddles,
Yolken dawns so green with yellow promise

And crimson sighs of yestersongs
Fevered fables of a bruised millennium
Tatooed by wars and scars
Wider than the map named for Atlas

Crossings
The moon's knock on the door of a stubborn era
And walls which heard moonsteps above the stoop,
Shadows of new comings

Footless winds, dreams without frontier
Misty intimations gray with grassy laughters
Above the bitumen feathers of asphalt soles
Hope soars on the road which came before the crossroads

Crossings
Migrations into new countries of the mind
New songs hatching on the ledge of the lip,
Eloquent door to the house of the mouth

A bucket of dew, a quarry of sunshine
Seasons which thresh our hold for grains
Of fresh harvests here where

Old twilights fade into younger epochs
Crossings
Festival of feet, flotilla of songs
A new millennium waits on the other side of the River,
Beckoning us over across The Bridge of Perfect Wisdom

9. 9. 99

9.	9.	99
flotilla	of	figures
number	ing	days
in	crowded	sameness
the	clock's	figured
face	glow	ing
in	chancy	awe
this	curious	quadruplet
from	Time's	amazing
womb	rare	like
a	millennial	mouse
time	ambles	in
diverse	digits	in
diverse	sea-	sons

STOLEN SILENCE

I

They are all gone now, the clan,
their shadows falling back
like the shawls of departing masquerades

the window opens its Venetian eyes
a flock of sunlight invades the room
night's remnants are in disarray

Visible now, things hitherto unseen:
a speck of dust on the larynx of a poem
cockroach wing on the tarmac of a fable

Soapsuds still hissing in the sink
on the bathroom mirror a strand of hair
bequeathed by a hasty comb

There is a gray stillness in the fireplace
pots hug their pans
dishes stand flat-bellied in the drainer

The couch wrestles the chair
for a piece of my brooding body
the desk beckoning with its inky fingers

A tingling silence engulfs the hour
long-sought, for ever expected
my nib itches for a blank page

II

Alone, magically alone,
I behold myself in the mirror
of my eyes

Garner silver echoes
from the murmur of lowering skies
reap the riot of fragrant acres

Waiting faucets drip crystal notes
in the symphony of silence
on walls white with paint

Footprints of ants on a lengthy journey
to the promised land in the cupboard
their laws are many, their scrolls severe

Ceilings have ears, talk in style
the roof hovers secure with its neon visage
the W.C. opens its bowel in a cascade of grunts

This silent moment, alone
I hear my heart's music in the chamber of an instant
I succumb to the inky beckon of my desk

MUSING BOULDERS

I have wandered through the imagination of stone
probed hard interiorities with the nib of a toe
and swayed to the cobbled tonality of the moon

Sculpted fables bloom into petals
a migrant poem drops in my lake of silence
drenched in song and murmurs

I have wandered through the imagination of stone
watched butterflies fledge into angels
angels into feathered marble

>   Can't you see their lift and thrust
>   their weighty soar through the empire of the sky
>   the harsh countenance of an outwitted sun

Wind-tranced, leaves rub their hands in prayer
the lizard nods a head red with pagan fire
the quarry talks back in blasts and ashen swagger

I have wandered through the imagination of stone
chiseled verse mellows into monuments
dreams simmer beneath the wit of musing boulders

BOOK OF ABSENCE

The waves roll up their trousers
and race towards the beach
like school boys on midday break

    Their uniform
    bubbling white
    upon a rippling blue

Crabs scramble in eyeless frenzy,
their clumsy scrawls
chalk fresh on a sandy slate

    The duck
    dips a feather
    in the tide

Scribbling tall tales with echoes
billowing from shore to shore
tossing the migrant alphabet of distant sails

    The sun
    beams its bliss
    from the socket of the sky

Sojourner,
I read it all
in the sea's blue book of absence.

POEMS IN PRISON

And the poem
in the prison house
of the book

    tongue-tied

scratching dotted spaces
pushing back imperial covers
s-c-r-e-a-m-i-n-g

    for an exit

ODE TO HATE

The journey from hate to holocaust
Is perilously short...

I know your name, oh Hate:
Memory's bastard
Trader in death and difference
Offspring of odious passions smoulder-

Ing like primordial geysers;
Author of flameless fires, waterless lakes
Words tipped with poison, flying free
In a gathering of innocent targets

You Hate are the permanent bellyache of the serpent
The cormorant which gobbles its own brood
Lizard with arsenic spittle
Funereal jaws of ancient dragons

Gaze of the salamander
Lipless teeth, coven of claws;
Your bed a cemetery of spikes
Headrest a pillow of scorpions

But you know no slumber, crave no rest
Your siesta is the sirocco, your hammock the hurricane
Wherever Evil parades its trumpet
You are a regiment behind its flag

II

Sometimes you are a mustached tyrant
Stiff as a swastika, mouthing fatal fables
Toasting blood in human skulls
Satanically insane, powerfully so

Sometimes you are a hooded thug
Lethal with loathing, burning crosses;
Or the snarling hyena at the school gate,
Blocking the way of the Children of Light

Other times you are the scaly Tribesman/woman
Dinosaur in your dreams
Wallowing in the blood of other clans
Betraying no sense, needing none

But I ask you, peddler of spurious purity,
Where do you live:
In the spleen, liver, heart, or head
Under the tongue, or in an eye

Which pierces like a vulture's talon
In the gorge, up craggy crests
In the icy wilderness, in desert dooms
In mean, rainless clouds or the grudging sea....?

I call your name, oh Hate,
Graveyard gallant, garden full of thorns
Trackless tears, wounds that never heal
You loom so large in the depths of darkness

Awaiting the searing ray of the human sun

A MODEST QUESTION (I)

The grass is busy growing in the fields
Every dawn with its dew is an immeasurable boon

The hedges spring wild around the garden
Begging giant clippers for a shave

The river wriggles along in the valley
Its upland boulders jostled into glowing smoothness

Bees are gathering nectar for their paradise of delight
The spider's loom is a factory of limbs

The early bird clears my eyes of its slumberous debt
Its beak so sure, its plumage laundered by distant rains

   Between thumb and finger I hold a seed
   Hard, dark-brown in the early sun
   Silent with History, smelling of the pod

   I let go; it revels in the wind
   Settling later in some soil of lime or loam
   Trying out its new bed, its pillow of pebbles

   The clouds send their rain, the sky its sun
   The seed becomes a tree, the tree a forest
   The forest an age...

If the grass is busy growing in the fields
And bees are gathering nectar

Why are men busy making war
And scattering the seeds of death

PURPLE SWAGGER[1]

They abandon the armory to the care of kids
Then strut back to their feathered bunkers
They cover their trench with a film of lies
Then summon our masquerade across their threshold of
tricks

    The arrow has quit its quiver
    Machetes have grown too large for their scabbards
    Can't you hear nuclear rumors erupting
    In the marketplace of our pain?

Caucuses by day, caucuses by night
Brazen dreams have set the sky on fire
Mayhems signed and sealed in silence
Have eaten the sun in a flash of rage

    And boasts the bully:
    I kill, therefore, I am...

Hands too full of arms cannot embrace humanity
Nuclear clouds have no silver lining.

---

2. This poem owes its inspiration and first appearance to *Depths of a Greyhound Terminal*, Alacrity Press, Boulder, Colorado, USA.

RWANDA

The lake runs red:
skull mountains prick the conscience of the clouds

Bloated vultures snore on remnant roofs
stench so strong it chokes the wind

A primordial monster usurps the land,
a mad machete in his hand

Shibboleths on his lips;
old scars fester into new wounds

The lake runs red

And the world watches the pogrom
from a long, lethargic distance:

Europe cannot locate the spot on the map
America cannot find a way through the jungle

And so blood trickles swell into floods
a distended earth bemoans a plague of corpses...

Once again, a dawdling world rallies
differently to the color of pain

The lake runs, red

THE LARGE HEART

When last did you say hello to a neighbor
Or share with him the early pick
From your backyard garden

When last did you lower that fence
Trim those thorny hedges
And throw a handshake across their forbidding top

When last did you stop in the street
To crack a joke or savor a banter
And spread the healing magic of laughter

When last did you say "Bless you"
To soothe a sneeze, or "Take care"
To one who has stubbed a toe

When last did you offer a meal
To a hungry stranger and command
The water from your well to wash his feet

When last did your dough of friendship
Rise in the furnace of the sun,
Your milk of mercy in the pitcher of the moon

When last did you think about your fattened calf
And the skinny swansong of the begging bowl
The sin-phony of your silk, and the scream of the national
rag

When last did you throw a bridge
Across the gulf
And sow little stars in the darkness of forgotten skies

When last did you listen to the wails of the forest
Arrest the savagery of a wanton machete
Enlist in the Salvation Army of Earth and Sky?

A genuine smile is longer than a mile
A large heart is not a medical problem

LETTER FROM THE EDITOR
(who once lectured a Nigerian poet of my acquaintance
    on the virtues of "traveling poems")

Thank you for your poems
Our Editorial Board was tremendously amused

But there are too many foreign places
In your verse, too many African names
Too strange for the sophisticated glide

Of our English tongue
(You see, we prefer words which pose
No threat to the dental health of our readers)

Too many matters better left to politics (and politicians)
What does poetry have to do
With those who rule us or those we rule

With the whimsical temper of stocks and shares
The cost of a ream of paper
Or the price of bread in the marketplace...?

Too strong, your feelings; too sharp
The thrust of your tropes
We are a people tuned to tamer truths

So, why not bend your wit to the rule of rhyme
The supremacy of nothingness
The post modernity of silence...

Send us poems unclogged by human kindness
Send us poems that travel

TEXT WORSHIP
(or the deconstructed passport of Traveling Theory)

Did you see the text pass this way
In coat and collar and pompous sway
A wizened Canon with the cutest creed
With a temple full of the bravest breed

Did you see the Text on the conference table
Talkative giant of a faddish fable
Pounding the podium, a mustached tyrant
How holy his sin tax, stupendously brilliant!

When I woke up this morning the Text was in my room
I aimed at its shadow, it held my broom
It jumped into my wardrobe, turned into a hat
Now I strut the streets with a trendy heart

It opens the door to the fattest jobs
The prettiest journals up for grabs
Arrange your jargon on a glittering rack
Your feet are firm on the tenure track

    Post-day post-night
    Post-history post-reason
    Post-humanist post-human
    Show me the post of your post-coloniality

    Aporia comporia catachresis
    Totalizing razmatizzing
    Meto nym nym nym logenctr tri tri tri
    Show me the structure of your post-structurality

Oh for a gram of Grammatogy!
    A sample sperm of Disseminations
    The Discourse tree with fruits of Discord
    And the New His-story-cism, New Her-story-cism

The madder the smatter, the harder the better
Make it new, make it arcane
The clumsier the code the sweeter the pain
It's the brave new era of the gaudy patter

Signs are here, the Word is dead:
The funeral of meaning a tropical debt
Paid in the surface of an idle game
In the dim-lit abyss of pedantic fame

Wars may rage, Hunger may spread
The river may die in its lowly bed
Chains may descend from every sky
The price of Freedom raised so high

Count your tropes, praise the Text
The meaningless meaning is a grand pretext
"Oppression" is merely undecidable reference
"Poverty" is slave to metaphysics of presence

The Author is dead, in unmarked grave dumped
The Reader to power with crown has rumped
The Text writes itself with a magic hand
In the curious way its priests can stand

It shouts in French, in English it whispers
It murmurs in German in gasps and whimpers
A Kingly silence in other tongues
The youngest heir to older wrongs

I bend my knee, oh mighty Text
Spare my days of your nightly test
Assure my path to your Temple of Awe
Let me rant while my listeners snore

ENTRY POINT ENCOUNTER

"What passport do you carry?"
"Nigerian"
"Nigerian?...oh please step aside"
I'll be with you in a moment"

    moments lengthen into minutes
    minutes into sweat-soaked eternity;
    my legs, tired of waiting,
    snap under my jet-weary body
    rooted to the polished coldness
    of an alien port;
    at last the passport man arrives,
    a plague of quizzes and queries

"How many hours is your "moment", Officer,
You've kept me standing here for ages:
I'm almost missing my flight"

    Silence
    Cold, imperial silence

"May I have your passport please?"

    I hand over my Nigerian nemesis...
    Scanning, laser-probe, laborious scanning
    a narrowing of eyes, twitch of the nose
    (There must be some green skunk in the jungle
    of a Nigerian passport)

"Your name?"
"Exactly the way it is in the book in your hand"

    A long, cold stare at the photo
    in the passport;

then another probing stare at the face
standing captive before the window

"What do you do for a living?"
"I am a writer, and professor of English"
"English? But you're Nigerian...African!"
"Yes, you can address your doubt
To the universities which awarded my degrees

   Face drops. Silence...

"Writer? What do you write?"
"Poetry, drama, prose, essays, and so on"
"Writer? I never knew, never thought, that em em em
I've never met... seen an African writer"
"Then right here, before you, Sir,
Is a practical cure for your illiteracy"

   Silence. Awkward silence...
   Instant reddening of contorted face

"So many visas in your passport:
why do you travel so often?"
"Because my writing takes me
To different places"
"You're Nigerian?"
"I thought I told you so"
"Have you ever been convicted of fraud?"
"No"
"Have you ever been denied a visa?"
"No"
"Has your passport ever been endorsed?"
"No"

   Pause

"You know that thing called 419?"[1]
"I've heard about it
But, I assure you,
If 419 and I meet in the street
We won't recognize each other"

   Hunmmunmm

"Have you ever carried illegal drugs
In your mouth?"
"No"
"In your ears?"
"No"
"In your skull?"
"No"
"In your stomach?"
"No"
"In your scrotum?"
"No"
"In your rectum?"
"Your question stinks, Officer"

   Silence. Awkward silence...

"What do you have in your bag?"
"Books, Officer. Books
And a few personal effects"
"What do you have in the books?"
"Words, Officer. Words"
"Eh?"
"Words, I say... Books...

Incidentally, one of them harbors
A poem titled "The Passportman at Hellsgate"

   Silence... An empty grunt

"Really, really? Interesting...

"Very interesting indeed!...
Officer, as you can see,
My flight is due in another...

Silence. Fidgety silence

"Are you married?"
"Yes"
"How tall is your wife?"

"Well, a couple of inches above your height"
"And children, how many?"
"I have long left that headache
To the Census Board"

Silence

"If I let you go, what's the proof
That you won't just melt away
And refuse to go back to Nigeria?"
"Simple, Officer,
Just tie a rope around my legs
And hold on to the loose end;
(Our ankles are no stranger
To such historic adornment);
Or, better still,
Plant an electronic beeper
In my stomach, so you can monitor...

Silence... Mumbling of muddled incoherencies

"Ok, ok,
Please wait while I speak to the supervisor;
I'll be back in a moment...

1. Also called "advanced fee fraud"; a notorious crime by which Nigerian
   fraudsters and their foreign collaborators cheat people out of their money
   through impersonation and fake deals.

BENEATH THE PRAIRIE MOON

To Cynthia Hogue
(after a reading of *Three Streets From Desire*)

We dance beneath the Prairie Moon
　　when the sun is somewhere south
　　　　gathering shapes, gathering shadows

When cows moo their mass
　　in the liturgy of milkyways
　　　　their udders heavy like unuttered prayers

We dance beneath the Prairie Moon
　　where memories breathe like chairs
　　　　in the vanished garden of forgotten tribes

Where dire-lects bloom into words
　　crashing through the capricious carapace
　　　　of imperial tongue arrest

We dance beneath the Prairie Moon
　　amid trampled dreams wafting like blues
　　　　through the metal windows of borrowed teeth

We dance beneath the Prairie Moon
　　where double-breasted Amazons
　　　　take back the night

Where women, not we-men,
　　unmake the terror
　　　　of violated virtues

We dance beneath the Prairie Moon
　　the sky our drum, swimming into the future
　　　　through the music of the wind

Beneath the Prairie Moon... we dance
five hundred years from Abundance
three streets from Desire.

SCRIBE OF THE TRIBE
(for Steve Arnold)

You dignify service with a loyalty
rare in this age;
duty being your diadem,
you honor every pledge

With a soul and style
only a stubborn faith begets;
Scribe of the tribe,
parchments come into bloom

Under the scrutiny of your nib
scrolls unroll, letters fall to earth
like golden grains in a season of Lean Cows
a herd of hieroglyphs grazes in the pasture of your palm

You were there when the day broke
and the sky glowed with the sunlight of our letters
your pen a roaring assegai,
you sailed through the alphabet of the mist

Yours are hands which gather
arms which embrace.
You endow Friendship with a new meaning
Love simmers in the fireplace of your breast

Old scribes never die
they simply mellow into griots
dipping veteran pens
in the inky depths of memory

We tease our debt to you
with a thousand songs and a thousand rainbows
you have done us "Honor"
in turn we chorus "Respect"[1]

1. Greeting custom in Jacques Romain's *Masters of the Dew*, a novel which
inspired one of Steve Arnold's most profound essays.

FOR ELDRED DUROSIMI JONES AT 71[1]

To the accompaniment of drums and flutes, the following song, essentially celebratory:

Call: Ìyẹyẹ́lúyẹ
Response: Alugbinrin
Call: Ìyẹ...yẹ...luyẹ o o
Response: Alugbinrin jàn ki jàn ki jàn alugbinrin

Your voice came across the oceans
with a ring of blue vowels,
consonants of liquid corrals

Scaling seven mountains,
stroking the sun-singed beard
of lowering eaves

Birds nest in that voice
with plumes of proverbs,
songs of endless seasons

Your voice came across the oceans;
I peruse its magic
through the window of the sky

    Ìyeyélúye...

    *   *   *

Pioneer, pathfinder,
you wielded a primal pen
through the dawn of our letters
when the first syllables toddled
out of trembling mists,
Black, inchoately anonymous;
a teething shiver wracked the spine
of the alphabet

1. Upon listening to his BBC interview with Hassan Arouni

till you doctored the haze,
proclaimed a name:

From Cairo to Isara
from Ogidi to Limuru
spectral fables swapped places with redolent songs
a rainbow feast was born,
the world was its large, ambiguous guest...

Hail the hand which nurtured these dreams
with its inaugural intelligence
its ingenious transplantations
its bold Adamic daring...
Hail him who nurtured the tendril into a grove

   Ìyeyélúye...

        *   *   *

Now twilight shadows are long
even where the sea bites the feet
of the Lion Mountain with a blue, Atlantic fury;
diamond laughters, sapphires of Sisyphus;
the burdens which shorten the necks

Of Othello's countrymen lie so imperiously
between a plundered past
and a present not so sure of its name;
maskless faces fall before the shrine
our memory is a toad which forgets its tale

Uncivil strifes, a cacophony of chains,
fat cows forage the pasture into lean seasons;
but Justice being his other name, my Scholar-Poet
plucks a line from Stratford's immortal bard:
let distribution undo excess...

And so, from the cemetery of our dreams
a compost of hope
sleeping seeds touched awake by a lyrical dew

our tears have (truly) cleared our vision:
FREETOWN shall justify the promise of its name

Ìyeyélúyee…

*   *   *

Live on, then, my Scholar-Poet,
Twilight shadows may be long,
who does not know that Life is stubbornly l-o-n-g-e-r?
Your vision now so internal, so eternal,
keeps capturing the bird on tomorrow's tree

Ripening rice fields dance towards your table
the raffia palm drops its honey
in the sanctity of your gourd
in your garden of a thousand fragrances
petals bloom into doves and rainbow spaces

Let rivers empty their burdens into the waiting sea
let the moon wane and wax
in the laboratory of its sky;
your liberal wisdom sews the seasons
into proverbs and silky laughters

Teacher, founder, author of humane letters,
Your drum throbs in the marketplace,
gathering metaphors and leaping visions
you who master the immensity of night,
arriving, still, with vistas of new dawns

Ìyeyélúye
Alugbinrin jan ki jan ki jan alugbnrin

(August 25, 1996)

35

FOR DORAH FUNMILAYO ROSEN

Shall I call you the tenacious flicker
Of the moon in a sky so thick
With lengthening shadows

Or the pliable gold
Of the sun in a dawn so brittle
With rays of tender stirrings

Shall I call you the answerable rain
In a season of long, long droughts
And the empty yawn of bewildered barns

Or a whisper
Louder than a thousand voices
A tongue which gathers the proverb of scattered tribes

Shall I call you a seed
Floating, floating in the wind
Stirring compost, a waiting harvest

    Goddess of Light
    Sixteen-flamed lamp of flowing rivers
    Matron of millet and magic

    The universe gathers under the foliage of your arms
    Your inventive laughter
    The untramelable span of your eyes

(Birmingham, Alabama, July 25, 1992)

FEATHERED HEELS
(for Mary-Lou and Don Burness)

Feathered, your heels
Through different skies
And oceans peopled by singing waters

Feathered, your heels
Through generous mountaintops
And valleys lush with answerable grass

Feathered, your heels
Through loinprints of resilient showers
And earth which rocks the cradle of a thousand dreams

Feathered, your heels
But back, always, to this earth,
Rooted like unfellable forests

II

From the skeletal memories of Yad Vashem
To the civilizing massacres of Abomey

From the plantain-pillared laughter of Buea
To the sea-drenched song of Poseidon's Temple

From the talking tombs of Montparnasse
To the oil-rigged swagger of Port Harcourt

This world is your canvass
Your dream a concert of intersecting lines

III

The pine-ringed majesty
of Lake Monomonac
busy squirrels
and morning doves hooting in
a distant sunrise

The polyglot wisdom
of this House of Dawn
where songs open the door,
their echoes audible on Monadnock peaks

In this house of word and bread
every wall is alive with that joy
which always is
on the other side of sorrow

(Rindge, April 1991)

FOR GEORGINA BEIER

Faces and masks   A galaxy of eyes
Masksandfaces   Spaces dense with polyglot dreams

Peoples. People   Ample-breasted
Long-limbed   Grove between the thighs

Slanted symmetries   Sky-blue laughters
Dimpled roundnesses   Pageant of yellow sighs

Fagunwa   Picasso

    A galaxy of eyes

    *   *   *

Your colors call us to a feast of life
From the liquid lyrics of Osun Osogbo
To the sandy echoes of Papua New Guinea

New forms wrestle ancient phantoms
Memory holds method by its gentle hand
Dancing gingerly across the canvas

    A galaxy of eyes

Rainbow forests, yes, yours are rainbow forests,
Lines crisscrossing like lianas
Undergrowths dark with green murmurs

Around those regions where a vigilant brush
Opens up purple windows to the sun
A wild strangeness mushrooms into multiple mouths

    A galaxy of eyes

A peopled imagination, dappled,
Under one sky a festival of voices
Indigo's indelible magic, a million

Threads in the active loom of being...
I ask Obatala for a name for you,
"Call her Yemoso[1]", the Wise One insists

(Bayreuth, September 1996)

1. Mother-of-Beauty

CHAVAKALI
(for Henry Chakava)

Cha Cha Chavakali High
Where fledgling stars groom their wings
For the journey to rainbow skies

History lives here: in the clear-soled footprints
Of alumni legends; in the boys who hatched into men
When dawn was chill and the sun's yellow yawn

Exploded from the misty top of Mount Kenya
Seeds sown so carefully at Chavakali have found
Fertile soil in the garden of a growing promise

Here dreams do not walk; they run:
Eager to catch the day, travel with the sun;
When discipline raises a song, diligence completes the chorus

Cha Cha Chavakali High
Aiming so high till you touch the sky
Your roots deep in our ebony earth

WAITING FOR THE RAIN
(For Hugh Masekela)

Your trumpet pumps the wind
with a bold, metallic roar;
the universe throbs in awe
a worsted thunder whines
in a blue corner of the sky

   Waiting, waiting for the Rain

Sound-mortars pound the stage
with the leaping idiom of forgotten tribes
their nouns glistening in the vineyard
of your cheeks, their ululations
tremulous like scars of millennial wounds

   Waiting, waiting for the Rain

Legends
of a mother's wail at the grave of an only child
of the shagging, shuggling trains of contract workers
of the ferocity of the whip in its boorish descent
of Sharpsville's blunt accent in Soweto's ears

   Waiting, waiting for the Rain

Memory hides in your song
in the sepia folds of a tune
which remembers its tongue
in the throat which bakes the bread
for our common feast

   Waiting, waiting for the Rain

Tambo's trek, Mandela's mandate
the lingering radiance of Ruth, ever First
the Spear of the Nation sailing,
sailing in the turbulent waters of your wind
beyond billboard rainbows, beyond, beyond...

    Waiting, waiting for the Rain

The Nile's long-limbed gallop
the limpid lyric of the Limp the Limp the Limpopo
the Kukuruku's tall whisper in the ears of the Kilimanjaro
the sun never sets in the empire of your song
your garland a forest of flowers and dappled murmurs

    Waiting, waiting for the Rain

Through paths of Fire
through dry undulations and epidemics of doubt;
in the wilderness of an epic still waiting for a tongue
your voice rises from the valley like swift eagles
teasing the slow generosity of the clouds

    History's bowl in our hands
    We gather the Rain

FOR BREYTEN BREYTENBACH
"An exile lives abroad like the moon in a pond"[1]

Moon in the pond,
you have danced the slow dance
of misty waters

Splashed milky shadows
on ripples trekking bankwards
for confirmations of alluvial dreams

Twilight, always twilight,
between clear tonalities
and dark intimations of

A sky dipping vigilant eaves
in the inky imagination of streets
sentried by difference

In the memory of their Snow
and their Dust there are thoughtprints
which weather a thousand gales,

Grafitti still dripping red
on the walls of slighted hearts
though each life is a novel

Each Memory a re-counted tale,
unforgetable pebbles line your return route
to a continent so inevitably ours

My long-traveled brother,
the moon in the pond will, one day,
turn a stone in clear water

HOPE never goes on permanent exile

1. Interview with Thomas Bruckner, Matatu, No. 11, 1994, p. 115.

THE BATTLE OF HASTINGS

The Zomba Butcher has crashed at last
After several seasons of bile and blood
Chingwe's Hole has swallowed in the end
A long-expected guest

It all happened in June,
Not even time for Mpina's Summer Fires
Though the nights were red all the same
With the delicious glow of water melon

A misty veil has dropped from Lake Malawi's face
Laughing ripples dance to
The ululations of the wind,
Hitting the long-suffering beach

In a hurray of beaded bubbles
In the purple magic of liberated seasons
There are songs which make water jump,
Which restore the leap to crippled joys...

Tell me, Jack,
Did the Chameleon change its hue
When faced with the verdict
Of a sorely abused forest?

Tel me, Frank,
Did you read him a few lines
Of "Ars Poetica" like a riot act
Even as he slunk, doddering despot,

Through the crackling canopy
Of Lupenga's foliage?
We will all be there with Felix
When sunset gracefully comes to Sapitwa

Welcome back from the Battle of Hastings
The scars run deep, the pains

Are rife. A new day breaks
Behind the Zomba mountain

We await its sun with vigilant joy.

FOR KOFI AGOVI[1]

I traded songs with the sea at Takoradi
And watched the boatmen return,
Their nets heavy with empty grief

The time was noon
The sun stood still in the center of the sky
Shadows were short and darkly dense

"Why trap the sun so in your glassy face?"
I asked the sea,
"Why have you seized the torch

Which puts the blaze in our fledgling hearths?"

The sea looked on in infinite silence
Even as I watched the boatmen return,
Their nets heavy with empty grief

I asked the crab
I asked the crane
I asked the gull with a salty whimper

Between its beak:
"My friend the boatman with a giant paddle,
When shall I celebrate his triumphant return?"

The minnows it was who turned my gaze
To the terrifying absence before my eyes
The boat was there, and also the paddle,

But my friend had vanished somewhere
Beyond the seas. I dipped my hand
Into my bag of memory, coming up
With missing gems:

His tall, intelligent gait, his broad-chested laughter,
That ebony sparkle on his cheeks...

    The sea looked on in infinite silence
    Even as I watched the boatmen return,
    Their nets heavy with empty grief

The *Winds From the North* this time
Are laced with whips of sand
Dusty scars mar the eaves, trembling, tremb-

Ling from the harm before the harmattan
The noontide sun suddenly done to dusk
In the infirmary of our anxious seasons

Brother, comrade, singer of tales,
I will take home the boat
And fashion it into a mighty flute

Your name
Will suffer no silence
In our house of songs

    The sea, the sea, looked on in infinite silence
    Even as I watched the boatmen return,
    Their nets heavy with empty grief

1. Late Ghanaian writer and academic; former Director of the Institute of African studies, University of Ghana, Legon.

DEATH CAME IN LITTLE WHISPERS
(for Ulla Schild)

Death came in little whispers
in a quiet crisis in the bones
in cells ambushed by hostile humor

Death came
in the pale hours before dusk
the harvest still ungathered

The arena waiting for a
festival of leaping songs
And then the skydog broke the moon

Like a tender bone between its teeth
the clouds reaped a tantrum
of bleeding twilights...

    We called one evening in the barnyard
    but your voice was already
    on the other side of the sky

That voice
tall as a proverb,
friendly as honey,

Which rang across three continents,
proclaiming the universality of our letters,
liberal Schild against the missiles of nescience

In a world sundered
by tongue and tribe
you are a stitch that never snaps

Sleep tall, Spirit of Light,
we shall kill Death
with the Memory of your generous Life

FOR TOM DENT

Call:	*Eni rere da'ra ile*
Response:	*Gbee gbee, òfèèrè, gbee*
Call:	*Tòómú lọọ, o digba*
Response:	*Gbee, gbee, òfèèrè gbee*[1]

Who will heal the tall sadness of your absence
　　The silences which astonish my ears
　　　　Each time my soul craves the solidity of your voice?
　　　　　　Where in the rafter did you leave that gourd of
wisdom
　　　　　　　　So brown with the moons, with the dust of sky
　　　　　　　　ways?

When you walked, your head teased the sun
　　Your crown a halo of golden petals;
　　　　Blessings dropped from your lips like ripe mangoes
　　　　　　You who tempered the tyranny of night,
　　　　　　　　Coming back always with blue dawns

And always this earth, our Earth, was your roost
　　You defended its trampled mountains
　　　　Raised the abandoned flowers in its valley
　　　　　　The wisdom of the wilderness exalted your garden
　　　　　　　　You listened mind-fully to the footsteps of ants

Ó se o pò, ó dun ni junrajinra[2]
　　The cock has crowed behind the man
　　　　The roof looks down from the sky
　　　　　　But the walls have lost the memory of their feet
　　　　　　　　Can't you hear the sorrow in the rasp of falling
　　　　　　　　leaves?

*   *   *

Down down down
Down River Road
The Mississippi's muddy magic

Glowing glowing glowing
In the evening sun;
Ah! the long, long tale of O? Man River

Flailing like a falling whip
Brown with sweat, blue with j-a-z-z
S-l-o-w as Pain
L-o-n-g as Memory
Shorter than H-o-p-e

Down down down
Down River Road
The crisp magic of Mississippi mornings
The funereal laughter of abandoned moments
Teeth white like cotton fields at harvestide

The fertile miracle of the Delta
where songs surge and fables flourish:
Its whiskered shoals
Paw prints of panthers
   The River, oh! the River
   The River is Sound
   The River is Silence
   The River is mask which confounds its Memory

Waters Waters…Waters of the Beginning
Of long, long nights and scarlet risings
Of darkness so heavy it cracked the egg of dawn
Light-footed fragrance of First Lights
Of murky clarities, veteran innocence of seeings/sightings

Waters of the Beginning
Of the rain
        rain
                rain
                        rain

Of the Cloud
  Which mothered the Rain
    The Rain which mothered the River
      The River which mothered the Sea
        The Sea which mothered our Pain

The rain
      rain
            rain
              Rain

Dimpling lake in gumbo pots
Showers of cheese flakes
Jamb   jamb   jambalaya
And chickens singing tasty ditties
In the curried choir of the feast

The rain
      rain
            rain
              Rain

In the liquid orgy of this amazing city
We seek shelter under the umbrella
Of the season's mushrooms

And other umbrellas spinning spinning spinning in the
   street
The saxophone's serpentine summon
The metallic b-o-o-m of the tuba
And rainbow floats and rainbow flairs

And the lyrical leap of sprightly revelers
And the primordial accent of the drum
                              the drum
                                    of the drum
                                          the drum

Ah! the Drum possesses
By whom is not the Drum possessed?

    *   *   *

Tòọ́mú dìde gìrìì, ojú ti mọ́
Àjànàkú dìde giirii, ewé ńjó lóko o o o[3]

Brother-Minstrel
When our Band danced through Treme today
I looked left, I looked right
Your door faced the street like a faithful sentry
But there was a grating silence behind the walls

   Tòómú dìde giirii, ojú ti mọ́

I saw your voice in the dialect of the Drum,
That tender drawl sometimes sharp like acid,
Free of cant, free of can'ts
Faith which never falters
Parable of the power which comes with Hope

   Tòómú dìde giirii, ojú ti mọ́

Wake up Brother-Minstrel
Unfinished mandates reek like rancid pledges;
Here, still, the staccato syntax of incontinent guns
Rips through the stupor of gangly ghettoes
Trapped still are we in the castle of our skin

   Tòómú dìde giirii, ojú ti mọ́

Wake up, Brother-Tom
The Free Southern theater throbs under
The primal echoes of Umbra;
River songs re-member their Blue Lights
Our Southern Journey has just begun

Call: Ẹni re d'ara ilẹ̀
Response: Gbee gbee òfèrè gbee
Call: Tòómú lọọ ó dìgbà
Response: Gbee gbee òfẹ̀rẹ̀ gbee

1. A good man has returned to Mother Earth
   Oh Good Winds, carry him on your wings
   Tom is gone, farewell
   Oh Good Winds, carry him on your wings

2. A great great pity, painful beyond recounting

3. Tom, wake up, the day has broken
   Mighty Elephant, wake up; the forest has broken into a dance

CHECKPOINT CHARLIE

A tortured rainbow:
mosaic of broken epics

Quarry for museum hounds
and undertakers for private temples

Here now in dust and concrete splinters,
the Wall which grew so tall, so wide

It cut the sky in two:
the sun rose on one side, set in the other

Market forces howled and swaggered on one side,
the whimsical Babel of stocks 'n shares

On the other, human Need wrestled with human Greed
culture with chaos, mercy with monopoly

Then, a smiling comrade dropped the egg
and the world couldn't gather the shattered pieces...

Our guide told the story from his own side
as I took another look at the boy

    who sold "The Wall" for tourist dollars

"Come buy History, come buy History!", he screamed
    again, his voice vanishing into the late morning traffic.

BERLIN 1884/5
"Come buy History! Come buy History"

I looked round for vendors of my own past,
For that Hall where, many seasons ago,
My Continent was sliced up like a juicy mango

To quell the quarrel of alien siblings
I looked for the knife which exacted the rift
How many kingdoms held its handle

The bravado of its blade
The wisdom of potentates who put
The map before the man

The cruel arrogance of empire,
Of kings/queens who laid claim to rivers, to mountains,
To other peoples and other gods and other histories

And they who went to bed under one conqueror's flag,
Waking up beneath the shadows of another
Their ears twisted to the syllable of alien tongues

Gunboats
Territories of terror...

Oh that map, that knife, those contending emperors
These bleeding scars in a Continent's soul,
Insisting on a millennium of healing.

ZIMBABWE (1)
(for the stone sculptors of Matombo)

And here
among the seeing stones of
Harare

Time's sole
glides on pebbled fables
and eloquent boulders echo

   the song of distant rivers

A chisel-handed moon
prospects rockscapes
for hints of rounded curves

An ebony laughter erupts
where steel meets stone
in a trimming fancy

   of answerable biceps

And the chips, once down,
are up where Freedom's l-o-n-g s-o-n-g
paved History's road

With crimson flakes
and bruised petals
of the heavenly

   flowers of Mutare

Here stones talk
in baobab idioms
and rooted ruins of Monomotapa.

(Harare, August 1991)

PRINCESS OF ASMARA

We talk about new flags and new flairs...

I stand tiptoe
On the edge of a sun ascending
But my hand cannot grab

The hem of your sky
Oh Princess of Luminous Beauty
Undo these shadows in

The valley of my memory
For ever bound by the poetry
Of your softness

Your keen, obstinate voice
And your hair billowing, billowing
Like rivers of a thousand nights

I stand, acolyte to your charm,
Your cheerful frown, the unheard musics
In the Red Sea of your heart, even as

We talk about new flags and new flairs...

(Erlangen, July 1993)

INVOCATION TO HONOR

    Honor will come home to me
    Naturally like feathers to the bird

I have washed my soul in the waters of Seven Rivers
Dived in on the dialogue of the Deep
And watched *Oluweri*[1] bestow her garlands
On a tribe of fluent swimmers

    Honor will come to me
    Naturally like feathers to the bird

I have pursued my dreams to the top
Of highest mountains, weathered roaring winds,
Cooled my brow with the mercy of the clouds;
I have beheld life's stories from the roof of toothless mouths

    Honor will come to me
    Naturally like feathers to the bird

I have walked the valley, hand in hand
With shrubs overlooked by haughty heights;
Clamorous in the shadows, rousing reeds to riot
Cultivating the laughter of the loam

    Honor will come home to me
    Naturally like feathers to the bird

I am skybound for the star of the seasons,
Clouds nodding, parting their misty waves;
I have courted the Moon, broken bread
With the sun, and fallen like a gentle shower
On an earth tormented by doubt and drought

Honor will come home to me
Naturally like feathers to the bird
I have worn the Emperor's chains like a necklace
Sowed smoldering syllables in the Garden of Silence
Assailed deaf walls with the battering ram of songs
Wherever Freedom raises its anthem
I am a stanza in its chorus

Honor will come home to me
Naturally like feathers to the bird

I am cousin of the Impala, husband of the Doe
Comrade of the Weaverbird, confidante of the Earthworm
The Limpopo lingers in my veins, the Mississippi in my
    memory
The Titicaca finds its cradle in the basin of my eyes
I am a restless warrior in the salvation army of the Earth

Honor will come home to me
Naturally like feathers to the bird

Agbe[2] never lacks a splash of indigo
Aloko[3] heals chapped seasons with the magic of cam
wood;
I have begged the egret for a quarry of chalk
Befriended the rainbow for a pageant of colors;
Akee seed, I glow in triumphant blackness

Honor will come home to me
Naturally like feathers to the bird

No one grudges the eagle for its mastery of the skies
No one rebukes the sea for the mystery of its depths;
The chameleon roves the forest with its wardrobe of hues
How many bowls can empty the Nile
How long the ladder that will reach the sky?

Honor will come home to me
Naturally like feathers to the bird
The beauty of the zebra is the symmetry of its stripes
The beauty of the gazelle is the lyric of its leap

The grace of *alapandede*[4] is the eloquence of its loops
Red red red is the magic of palm oil
Tó tó tó is the music of life's water

Honor will come home to me
Naturally like feathers to the bird

A well-spoken word is the bride of the ear
A well-laundered sun is the glory of the sky
Well-spun threads are the pride of the loom
A flotilla of feathers is the splendor of the peacock
A character free of evil is the beauty of the human being

Honor will come home to me
Naturally like feathers to the bird

The elephant is no object for a meager glance
The rainbow stands out of a parting in the clouds
I stand solid on a plinth made of dawn
Sweetness has no foe in the house of honey
My covenant is Light, Light my eternal consort

Honor will come home to me
Naturally like feathers to the bird

Yíyẹ yíyẹ yíye ni nyẹyẹlé[5]
Dídè dídè dídè ni ndàdàbà lórun[6]
The giraffe never begets a dwarf
There are no bitter tales in the house of honey
Ire loni, ire lọla, ire nla ire gbẹ̀ngbẹ́ẹ́ẹ́ẹ́ẹ́[7]

Honor will come home to me
Naturally like feathers to the bird

1. Water Spirit
2. A Bird with a deep blue plumage
3. A Bird with a red plumage
4. A swallow
5. Honor walks in the company of the pigeon
6. Comfort is the mate of the dove
7. Goodness today, goodness tomorrow, ample, ample goodness

From
Horses of
Memory

MEMORY'S ROAD
(for many voices, in orchestra)

Chariots of dew arrive with horses of hills,
hoofs of woolen clouds. Spurs are fires of quickening
    kilns

the wheels gliding balm on memory's spine
The road, the road is thread of hair
  half-black   half-white
in the running stitches of earth and sky

Thread of hair thread of air
in the pealing cackle of rain and thunder
in the misty whis per of sea and sand

The hair twines into a snake
  half-black   half-white
with a tail of liquid lanes

And the snake demurs, heavy with sizzling marvels
loved last season (and the season before)
by the nodding fire of heel and hoof

                 *

And the snake, hesitant still,
falls one morning
on the brow of the forest;
and snakelets, mortally tired
of the prison of the womb,
eat cleanly through
the frail hide of a startled mother

Resplendent in foetal blood, they
wriggle different ways
like offsprings of a scattered pod:

67

some twine into lanes
narrow and well trodden;

some open into alleyways

where moon meets night
in whispers and throbbing breaths;
some twine into loops
where head is tail
and tail is head;
others throw open the farmward path
where the farmer's sole, shoeless,
telegraphs blood and brawn
to the laterite temple of pulsating earth
And paths and lanes and alleys
    meeting
labor in mud and dust and dirt
till, at long intricate last,
the crossroads is born...

*

Meet me at the crossroads
where the road wears trousers
of uncountable legs

Meet me at the crossroads
where earth marries sky
and the sun locks his horn
with twilights of prancing knights

Meet me at the crossroads
where raging fire breaks the teeth of iron
before joining steel to steel
in spiderworks of urgent flares

Meet me at the crossroads
where strand crossing strand

yields a barn of rapid looms

Meet me at the crossroads
where fact mating fancy
spawns tapestries of strangered truths

    And here the crossroads

    where the Trickster Prince
    counts tangled moments
    in laughter and dappled tears

    And this the crossroads
    godstop in dust
    right of polyglot pass-age

    *

Passage
of latticed visions,
compass of pointed probings

Passage
of bows and bends
of oiled elbows of tall journeys

Passage
of mamba ditches
pythons of sneaky craters

Passage
of white shadows reddening
in speedy coffins and syncopated dreams

Passage
of tear-drawn hearses
and parasols of ashen eaves

Passage
of headward burdens
stopping short at the knee of noon

Passage
Of wit and wind
of images wrestling words in mind-tunnels

    *

The Road crosses the River
The River crosses the Road.
And, bristling with lengthy rage,
The Road says to the River:

    "See, you boneless serpent,
    See what you have done
    To my supple frame"

And says the River, in rapid retort:
    "You saddle without a hill
    You hoof mat for pissing brats
    Never deem me the pain
    In your broken joint
    I am the sea which predates the hill,
    The slender honey in the eye of the gods"

The Road puts forward his ashen head
The River lays bare her missing teeth;
They count the strands, they count the holes
They find no answer to the riddle of age
They call the Earth, they call the Sky
They ask each sage their season of birth

To speak first is Earth,
Her fingers still quick with clay;
She who is earth, earth her memory.

"You Road are older then the River
You Road are younger than the River
You are as old as the dust in the wind
The fire in the tail of the parrot
The ring on the finger of the tree;
You were born after the River
You were born before the River"

Clearing his throat,
The Sky says with the metallic finality of Osanyin[1]:
  "You River, you are older than the Road
  You River, you are younger than the Road:
  You are the adamantine tears of stone

  The silent ears of primeval sounds
  The million stitches in the garment of the chameleon.
  You were born after the Road
  You were born before the Road"

Confused,
Road and River rage on in a cloud of doubt;
They ask the eagle, they ask the hawk;
They ask the vulture whose beak
Is death that never dies.
They ask, oh how they ask!
The more they ask, the older they grow
They ask till their questions ripen into answers
They ask till their answers re-form into questions

They ask
And the Bridge answers
In stratagems of steel
Tongues of steaming mortar
Incantations of fire stone;

The Bridge, ah the Bridge!
The Road takes off his clothes

Upon your iron bed,
The moistening waters below
Alive with seminal breaths.
But if the Road looks down upon the River
Once upon a lofty platform,
Let it not forget the stream waiting noiselessly
Behind the hills
Far, far below the belt of the forest

Ears of steel, eyes of mortar,
The Bridge is the god
Who looks back by looking forward,
Coupler of sundered wanderings

And looking back,
The Road sees a cavalry of dust
Laying low the tyranny of the hoof.

And says the Earth:
   "You Road, you are older than the River
   You Road, you are younger than the River"

(Yaddo, August 1986)

1. Yoruba god of magic and medicine.

MEMORY STREET

The juggernaut has broken the teeth
of the street
broken the teeth of the street
The juggernaut has broken the teeth
of the street
ancient molars litter the lanes
of our bleeding memory

    where now the laughter of the eaves
    where now the children who pulled
    the beard of the road?

The juggernaut has broken the teeth
of the street

    where are the dancers who lost their legs
    to the frenzy of the drum;
    where are the houses which wore their windows
    like frozen ears
    where are the doors which sprang a throng
    of open arms?

The juggernaut has broken the teeth
of the street

    down the road, under the baobab
    behind the wall where shadows rose and fell,
    the forge once spoke in syllables
    of steel and silence
    just one hearth throw from the corner
    where wordsmiths once passed round
    the kola of wisdom

The juggernaut has broken the teeth
of the street

    the market rose with the sun

    captured the blue center of the sky,
    then plunged with the skeletal shadows
    of deserted stalls

The juggernaut has broken the teeth
of the street

    the juggernaut has come
    with a cacophony of edicts
    the edict ate the street
    the street ate the houses
    the market ate itself...

The juggernaut has broken the teeth
of the street

    the juggernaut ate the memory of the street
    the edict ate the season of the moon;
    and when tomorrow comes with galloping thunder,
    what will the street say became
    of the tree with the golden root?

The juggernaut has broken the teeth
of the street
The juggernaut has broken the teeth
of the street
ancient molars line the lane
of our bleeding memory.

(Yaddo, August 1986)

74

SCARS OF UNREMEMBRANCE
(for Harry Garuba)

(to the accompaniment of kora, bata, and and/saxophone)

We summon our scars
We summon our scars
to this great gathering
of bleeding shadows
We summon our scars
to this harvest of lesions

    We summon our scars
    But where are the wounds?

We summon our scars
in the clearing of
forgotten jungles
We summon our scars
in the twilight
of slumbering masks

    We summon our scars
    But where are the wounds?

We summon our scars
from the fainted fall
of distant waters
We summon our scars
from rains which came and went
in the wake of oblivious roofs

    We summon our scars
    But where are the shadows?

II

We summon these scars
in the infirmary of amnesic spaces

We summon these scars
in the blood which clotted into stony orders
We summon these scars
in ears of lipless drums
We summon these scars
in a colony of tale-less toads
We summon these scars
in the fold of mountains
losing track of the valley
We summon these scars
in the chamber of the mouth
which forgets its tongue

    We summon our scars
    But where are the wounds?

We summon our scars
like rude interruptions
in the dialogue of the skin
with no crossroads of remembered hurt

III

To look is not to see

The scars those scars
printed so cruelly on the pages
of our mind
The scars those scars
rings of broken tissue
prophets in the wilderness
of our skin

To look is not to see

76

IV

Unheeded,
Memory's drums;
And our fire throws open its door
to perennial drenchings,
our shepherd lays out his flock
for wolves of clever twilights

I sing of ankles long oblivious
of the appetite of the chain
I sing of ankles long oblivious
of the appetite of the chain

I bide you,
Memory,
you who suture the moons of disparate skies

    We summon our scars
    But where are the wounds?

WE SHALL REMEMBER

We shall remember
We shall remember
The drought which ate the vulture's forest
And left a scar on its head

   We shall remember
      the plague which left a sore
         behind the bullying baboon

We shall remember
We shall remember
The fire which danced last season
Leaving tongueprints on the apron of the jungle

   We shall remember
      the saddle of the horse
         which adores its burden

We shall remember
We shall remember
The sun which forgot its ears
In the chambers of the clouds

   We shall remember
      the toad which lost its tail
         in a race of limbless leaps

We shall remember
We shall remember
The street which grew so long
It forgot its name

   We shall remember
      the flute which left its lips

      in a town of mouthless giants

We shall remember

We shall remember
For the hunchback cannot forget his burden.

.

AFRICA'S MEMORY

I ask for Oluyẹnyẹtuyẹ bronze of Ife
    The moon says it is in Bonn

I ask for Ogidigbọnyingbọnyin mask of Benin
    The moon says it is in London

I ask for Dinkowawa stool of Ashanti
    The moon says it is in Paris

I ask for Togongorewa bust of Zimbabwe
    The moon says it is in New York

I ask
I ask
I ask for the memory of Africa
The seasons say it is blowing in the wind

    *

The hunchback cannot hide his burden

SKINSONG (2)

My skin is the color
of earth
the smell of the rain
within the embrace of the flower;
rivers which echo the steps
of distant mountains

   I am dawn
   which succeeds the night

I live in the laughter
of your ribs
the energy of a guffaw
riding the crest
of a million sorrows

I gather your tears
in the darkness of my hands
and a river erupts
which irrigates
a century of laughing roots

SKINSONG (3)

And pale shadows descend
Upon our noon of bronze:

"You have no past", they say,
"Your history is darkness
Which never knew the faintest sun"

"Tell us another lie",
Retort the griots,
About trees without roots,
Rivers without sources
Becauses without whys
Tell us
About the bridge
Which looks forward
Without a backward glance

END OF HISTORY

Old truths tumble down
In sunrise cities;
A hated wall dissolves
In a haze of fireworks
And gathering shadows

Old truths tumble—
On the compost of newer Truths

And sunset pundits swear
They have climbed the mountain
And seen History's grave
In the elbow of misty valleys

Pundits say
The sun has suddenly stopped
Its limbless journey across the sky

Today I look History
In the face,
His/her brow a taut membrane
Of inexhaustible riddles

Today I look History
In the face
And I remember the child in the tale
Who touched the elephant's tail,
Vowing he had seen everything
About the giant of the forest

TENDER COURAGE

You are, also, the lingering echo
Of Nzinga's laughter
When she spat native venom
In the conquistador's consuming eye

You are the tender courage
Of Yaa Asantewa
Who trapped roaring bullets
In the hem of her wrapper

The sea's womb is forge
For answerable strivings
The hand which rocks the cradle
Also pulls the trigger of Memory's gun

GREEN MEMORY

Memory, too, is
the footsteps of ants
in the corridors of the forest,
the winged termite's fleeting frolic
in the wake of the first rains
the squirrel's fly-wisk tail
in the province of nutty seasons

Memory is
the penetrating touch
of the January dew
the dusken fluff of the homing eagle...

Shake hands with a tree today
Share the memory of a river

MEMORY'S MASK

You gave me
Memory,
And then a mask

With a thousand eyes
To pierce those undulating mists
Behind your Mountain of the Moon

To thresh every cloud
For grains of blue showers
Then kill several suns

At the elbow of the hill
Counting petals of the mercy
Sprouting in your bed

Of early rains.

Yours, too,
Is a peopled imagination:
I can summon those lost arks

In the covenant of your palm,
Fearing no angry prophecies
Nor floods of partial gods

TESTAMENT (1)

I hold this shred of eternity
in my hand
pulsating like a purple pledge;
falling leaves twirl in the soundless wind
the sun brightens up its corner of the day

The after-noon bell has come and gone,
burying rapid moments in decibels of silence

I hold this shred of eternity
in my hand

I sew that thread
into the memory of the sky
where clouds are cottonballs
waiting for the lyric of the loom

I am a poet:
my memory is a house
of many rooms

VICTIM OF A MAP

I, too,
am victim
of a map
which forgets its land:
phantom mountain
and
rivers without names;
object of an empire whose sun
once set in the east
of bleeding spears

NIYI OSUNDARE

WHO'S AFRAID OF THE PROVERB?

(*To go with the song:*
Owe lẹsin ọrọ
Ọrọ lẹsin owe
Tọrọ ba sọnu
Owe la fi nwa[1])

I

Who's afraid of the proverb
   of the eloquent kernel in the pod
     of silent moons

Who's afraid of the proverb
   of the kola in the mouth of the mountain
     giant udder of the cow of the sky

Who's afraid of the proverb
   of the drum which left its echoes
     in the auricles of leaping streets

Who's afraid of the proverb
   of the river which traverses the earth
     in limbless intensity

Who's afraid of the proverb
   of the sonic feathers of metaphors in flight
     the lift and thrust of impossible fancies

Who's afraid of the proverb
   of the wind's truthful lyre
     melodic thrum of Desire's fingers

Who's afraid of the proverb
   of the shortest distance
     between many truths

89

II

Who's afraid of the proverb
who so fat on the Lactogen of the moment
has lost all hint of the milk of dawn

Who's afraid of the proverb
who so drunk on the cant of imported parrots
has no ear for the dialect of the drum

Who's afraid of the proverb
stalking minnows in brackish waters
scared of the shoals which surprise the deep

Who's afraid of the proverb
anonymous spaces
in the abyss of the sky

Who's afraid of the proverb
first clay in the furnace
of chilling fires

Who's afraid of the proverb
silent salt in the feast
of delicious words

Who's afraid of the proverb
who's afraid of
m-e-m-o-r-y?

1. The proverb is the horse of the word
   The word is the horse of theproverb
   When the word is lost
   It is the proverb we use for finding it

ON READING SENGHOR, AGAIN

Those mellifluosities
From Sine to Seine
Shiploads of stars
On cataracts of liquid dreams

A vast anonymity of sleep
Stirred by the ancestral clarion
Of the *kora*:
    Dance dance dance
    Dance ye maidens of Wailing Waters

A night full of suns
Has captured the dark tonalities
Of dispossessing skies

Chaka's blood-stained laughter
In the armpit of striking spears
Pale intimations of orphaning storms
And the profound sadnesses
Of nights without dreams
    Without dreams
    Of nights without dreams

Those mellifluosities,
Oh bard of sonorous silences,
Those labyrinths in the castle
Of the drum
    Of the drum
    Of the drum

Spring proud recrudescences
From a baffling past:
A past, alas, lying at the crossroads
Of a sternly ambiguous journey

Sing sing sing
Oh Maidens of Rainbow Nights

Sing of perfumed silences
Sing, too,
Of panthers about to pounce
   About to pounce
   About to pounce

PEOPLED IMAGINATION (4)

Mine is a peopled imagination

Of voices from forgotten seas
whose spices sweeten the steps
of passing moons

Of nubile hills
whose tender miracle
is feast for every eye

Of songs from remembered fables
and trees which wear their forests
like magic robes

In the marketplace of my eyes
memories jostle for right stalls;
a friendly uproar crests the dust

   of nomadic heels

My masks are many; un-
countable sunlights name every line
of my figured face

I MET HISTORY TODAY

(Preferably in two alternating voices, one female,
the other male, with musical accompaniment)

I met History today
Between the first lights
And the last brief flickers of an ancient sun
I met History
In the void where bold-toned rainbows
Share mapless borders
With migrant clouds

I met History today
where Road crosses River
On a bridge of iron shadows
I met History
On the Mountain of the Moon
Ticking red, red, blue
In volcanic Eternity

I met History today
Draped in purple robes
And jewels from distant seas
I met History
A scarecrow in ragged echoes
Abandoned in the afterglow
Of fugitive harvests

I met History today
In gray wig
And gravest gown
I met History
Bound and battered
In the quibbling dock
Of accidental Pilates

I met History today
Her eyes blue
With Atlantic fire
I met History

Harvesting silent fields,
His hand a pale dungeon
Of seething whips

*   *   *

Petals in the storm
Fragrance of absent gardens

Rocks which beat back
A thousand waves

Deserts wild
With insistent harvests

Mountains which flow
In crimson ripples

Waters burning
Like angry oils

Gulf
Bridge

*   *   *

I met History today
A dove hovering around
His civil head
I met History
Trigger-ready
In the saddle
Of rugged accents

I met History today
In the chariot
Of galloping Pharaohs
I met History
In the ranks
Of fleeing tribes

Desperate for a parting in the sea

I met History today
Silicon marvel
From a galaxy of chattering chips
I met History
Simian effigy
With a cache
Of seething skulls

*   *   *

I met him, a shark
In the sea of clouds
I met her, a lion
In the jungle of pink shouts

I met him, a thread
In the eternity of a wink

I met her, an ocean
In the bowl of a week

*   *   *

I met History today
At the
Crosssssssroooooooaaaaaddddddsssss
I met History
Swaying mask

Of remembrance
And forgetting

I met History today
A wilderness
Of silent shadows
I met History
In a diaspora of voices
Raw, deep, insistent
Beyond recounting

HORSES OF MEMORY
(with horns, strings, drums, etc., medley of voices)

> *Ride me, memory*
> —Kofi Awoonor

I
Hoofthrongs awake my ears
A legion of hints has come,
Spraying petals of distant flowers

Hoofthrongs on memory's trail

Hoofthrongs quicken the eagle of my eyes
A feathered sky descends
Lending flight to uncollected visions

Hoofthrongs on memory's trail

Hoofthrongs blacken the page of whitening sheets
A multitude of alphabets arrives
Scribbling blood into pale musings

Hoofthrongs on memory's trail

Hoofthrongs stir the sleeping drum
A tannery of voices alights
Speaking flairs of eloquent thunders

Hoofthrongs on memory's trail

II

The rain, the rain is
memory of the drought:
every drop there is
is memory of the grain that was

98

Ah! The dew is the memory of the dust

And the Grey One unrolls her mat of wisdom:
   "People of our land, what were you doing
   what were you doing, people of our land?
   when earthworms twined into sudden cobras
   what were you doing;
   why no hint of the first cobra
   who just last season gobbled our priceless eggs?"

The desert, the desert is
the memory of the sea;
every grain there is
is memory of the drop that was

   III

Shadows across the path
the masquerade smells absent moons
in the trail of fleeing shrouds
shadows across the path

There are singing embers
in the rubble of yester-fires;
an ashen prophecy unbinds the Word
in crucibles of remembered visions

The roof re-calls footsteps
of departed showers
an itinerant lightning reminds the sky
of the sanctity of untrodden tracks

The egg, the egg, is
the memory of the hen;
every chick there is
is memory of the yolk that was

IV

The bushfowl in the roadside grass
is the hunter's puzzle:
it hears with its beak

its every feather is a galaxy of eyes

The ram wanders without remembering
it becomes an instant guest of the butcher knife;
the antelope jumps into an open trap,
wondering why it left its eyes at home

The nanny goat forgets its head,
whipped countless times for repeated offences;
there is a simmering tale, still,
in the hearth of a thousand seasons

Shadows across the path
Shadows, in the tell-tale whisper
of corrugated echoes
the hill gathers a harvest of songs

Oh memory,
eye of the road,
nose of running rivers
hoofthrong of departed horses

V

(strings, horns, drums, and voices in final flourish)

Ride me, then, memory
Ride me on the saddle of your eyes
Looking back, looking forth
Like the bridge of musing waters

Ride me through troughs of terror
Through rivers of bristling fires
Ride me through shadows of forgotten suns
Through larynx of echoing hills

Ride me through the summon
Of clashing cymbals
Ride me through the membrane
Of jubilee drums

Ride me like the fire

Joining seasons of steel
To seasons of molten laughter
Ride me, Memory...

From
Midlife

From ROCKSONGS

i

am a caller at noon
restless sphere of the universe of the sun,
of galloping oceans and rocks
which bathe their feet in misty waters,
of the sky's blue, blue teeth
and clouds which gather the promise of rain

I am light
I am shadow
I am the luminous covenant
Of short and tall spaces

I am the eye's mid-wink
in an orchard of visions,
depths which find their name
in the register of brightening dials

I am the green rhumba of the forest,
of tapping roots, and twigs
swaying, swaying to the promptings
of the wind,
an echo passed tree to tree
like a legend of whispering idioms;
I am the amber sheen of coconut leaves
rasping, rapping in the theatre
of the breeze,
the long hard journey from crust to core

I am the luster of the river
in the swollen plenitude of August;
banks which count their coins
in shadows of rapid showers

I am a caller at noon;
I have cut my teeth
at the elbow of the moon;

ripening cornfields drive no fear
into the mouth of my sun

I am a caller at noon.

   iii

Through burning waters
Through ashes of accumulated patience
Through earth which chews the showers
of tardy rains
Through lakes pregnant with storms
Through seasons which bloom every seed
For twilights of contending baskets
Through earth's gable
Through the window of the sky

   The sun reaches out for its ram horn[1]

Waiting noons are auricles of radiant blarings;
my memory now is a tale of a thousand masks
I am a caller at noon.
I look the sun, my sun
in the face
and I harvest colors of unnamable depths
where sowing, once dew, now sweat,
is shade for a million temples.
Light is my promise
my shadow hemless ripple
of the ocean's abiding loom.

The seed, once dew, now sweat,
the dripping clay of the first light

has hardened into a polished porcelain
of thickening shadows

I am light
I am shadow
I am the luminous covenant
Of short and tall spaces

I am a caller at noon

iv

Child of the river, child of the rock
child of the delicate boulder
of the beginning,
of burning quarries and flames
of eloquent clay

Cinders of the first fire
cinders, of the first scarlet sprinkle
and murmurs of parting mists,
of the telling legacy of the blaze
which swallowed the night,
spitting flint and flair
in paths of hardening lores

   The boulder is father of the rock
   The boulder is father of the rock
   Swift-footed courier of the craggy acre
   The egg which crows the tale
   In cradles of ashen dawns...

And, sizzling from the sun,
from the first blue touch of the waiting sea
the boulder cools its fine-grained heels
in the liquid mercy of rippling dusks

My coming is a continent
Without a frontier,
The boulder is father of the rock.

Child of the river, child of the rock
child of the rock which lends flying flakes
to pagan winds;
the flakes fashion different legends
in diverse lands:

some spring into domes

some into temples
some into steel-legged pillar
of the bridge in the belly of the river

    some into gold
    some into diamond
    some into multiple stars
    in the firmament of stone

some into castles
some into towers
some into statues which ply their tale
in regions of lenient showers

    some into lyric
    some into song
    some into sculpted flute
    in the hand of whirring winds

some into *gba*
some into *gbu*
some into the *gbaagbuu*
of *Mehunmutapa*

    The boulder is father of the rock

108

The boulder is father of the rock
of sibling slabs lying back to back
in the family of rooted walls

The boulder is father of the rock.

v

I am child of the river, child of the rock
Child, of rocky hills holding hands
Above the tallest roofs.
Dawns are gray, dusks brown:
Whoever craves the blue legend of Ikere skies,
Let him turn his neck like a barber's chair,
For here the rock is earth, the rock is sky;

Squatters we all on the loamy mercy
Of generous stones

For here the rock is yam
I am child of the river, child of the rock
Of the elephant rock which sleeps
In the eastern sky;
It snores in showers,
The early sun breaks its egg on its sturdy rumps.
I am the yellow yawn of its first hours,
Its red, red nod in hours of homing hues.

I am child of the rock
Too high for the legs of the eye;
For the elephant is feast for any sight
Ah! The elephant is feast;
Whoever takes the jungle's giant
For a passing glance
Craves trampling mortars in his tender farm,
The elephant is feast for any sight

I am child of the rock,
Of the lofty loins of *Ugelemotirimo* [2]
Who fathers seven broods,
Still seeking the scent of passing maidens.
Oh what ribaldry, the poetry
Of romping seasons:

> The okro penis which irks the hungry wife,
> The tireless cunt which swallows a log,
> Still craving a pestle for an itching corner,
> The whistle and baton under the warder's
> baggy shorts,
> The hidden treasure in the school mistress's
> chalk-encrusted skirt

> *Gboo-gbaa labara labara*
> *Gboo-gbaa labara labara*
> Testicle of the ram
> The ewe's feast, the shepherd's pride

> Swinging in the wind
> Swing swing swing swing
> It's swinging in the wind
> *Gbo-gbalabara labara*
> Testicle of the ram

Yours is the season
Of barns let loose in palm oil,
Of *efinrins* [3] sniffy courtship of the bride
Of the nose,
Yours is the stalk which tearfully
Yields its cob to the starving hand,
Pumpkins which roll in the furrows
Like a harvest of juicy raptures.

I am child of *Ugelemotirimo*
Whose foot is tricky with wet earth
Where wrestling limbs grapple,
And heelmarks echo the wail
Of fallen manhoods.
The season's clay sticks to the memory
Of my toes,
But my back, like the cat's, is clean;
I who leap through the seasons,
Bound to spring, never to lie.

1. Ram-horn: the visionary's medium, used for calling tunes and for
   rallying good will.
2. *Ugelemotirimo*
3. A plant with mint-like smell whose leaves are used as spice.

From WHAT THE RIVER SAID

(*Ibembe* drums, *sekere*, then the song:
Call! *Ẹ jọwo ẹ ma ta yẹpe si o*
Response: *Ẹni ọwọ lẹyẹleee...*[1])

i

Child of the rock, child of the river
Child of the river which plies
The world with hidden legs;
Offspring of the mountain
Mother of the rain
Fair of frogs
Roost of happy shoals.
The rock knows the rhythm of swaying water
The rock knows the rhythm of swaying water
Joyful antimony in the eye of the rain-washed paths
The rock knows the rhythm of swaying water

Ẹma ta yẹpẹ si o

The river has a song
Oh the river has a song
Pigeon-white, the lyric of the valley
In seasons when lowlands floods
Are red with upland clay
And the Maiden, chalk-spotted,
Sways under the compelling benedictions
Of the calabash bowl!

The river has a song
The river has a song
Deep-timbred tenor of whispering forest,
The raffia suckles its roots,
Its udder springs a lake of honeyed wine.
Bring the keg, bring the gourd

112

Bring healthy throats so smooth
With the traffic of flowing songs
The pigeon is white, so the wine,

And so this clay from the quarry

Of supple memories
The wine is white
And black, black runs the earth
At the palm's tenacious root
The river has a song

    Ẹ ma ta yẹpẹ si o

The river has a song
The river has a song
Balm on burning brows
Master of the flame
Murmuring tunnels which wash dawn's face
With a bowl of clouds.
The sky is your depth,
Every boulder bears a womb
Of scarlet flowers

    Ẹ ma ta yẹpẹ si o

Let me go down with you,
Ageless river,
Behind the trees,
Near the big toe of the hill
Where naked water taunts

The pride of the sponge
And droplets traverse the folds
Their hearts upright like throbbing dreams.
Between sand and water,
In the flower of the water-cress
Which bats the eyelid of waking puddles,
I sound out the shrill of the shell,
My ears pluck the whispers of spotless depths
I walk back home,
My feet chaste like a righteous pledge

Ẹ ma ta yẹpẹ si o

The river has a song
The river has a song
Sun, moon, stars, hills, trees,
The *tiuntiun*[2] which wings its way
Across a blazing noon,
Echoes of the village ballad

Remnants of the city noise
Rumors of the king's fortunes
Tales of the queen's goiter
All so tellingly mirrored
In the palm of the river.

The river is in my eyes
My eyes are in the river
Ah! The river has a song

Ẹ ma ta yẹpẹ si o

I am child of the river
Child of running streams
Which have no harbor for stagnant death
May the season be a pod of many seeds
May the season be a pod of many seeds

The river has a song
The river has a song

The song has a river

E̩ ma ta ye̩pe̩ si o

1. Do not spatter it with mud
   the pigeon is a sacred being
   (The pigeon is Osun's favorite bird)
2. A very small bird with a sharp note

From HUMAN IN EVERY SENSE

I am caller at noon
the hole of that key
the key of that door
the door of that house
the house of that street
the street of that town
the town of that country
the country of that world
where rooms are large
and a smiling yam whispers yes
to every hunger;
I am also the hinge of eternal windows;
the spine of the book of life.
So when you walk, never bruise your shadow:
I am the pearl of your laughter,
the watering passion of your garden of tears

I am the speck of dust in the evening air
bubbling butterfly in the estate of the flower,
kite in a mellow sky,
foe of the storm, friend of the wind,
if I come near your mirror
I am instantly a lavender of eternal fragrance
if I settle near your garden
I am loam of immeasurable promise;
touch me with the dew of a generous dawn
and I turn talkative clay in your molding hands.
I am cactus, veteran of stubborn mercies,
mining fluent chatter from the accent
of ancient sands,
porcupine though my masks,
my limbs a patient tablet of pilgrim scrawls:
polyglot my joy, my tattoos desperate vows
of fleeting lovers.

I am the forest of the desert
the stem of every sand, branch of every speck,
giant moss on the brow of the dune,
amazingly green;
I am the wind which sculpts the sand
into magnificent patterns
I am the bridle of the sandstorm: I steer
the sirocco's savage horse from tracks
of wanton ruin.

I look through the sand, I see a fountain,
I look through the fountain, I see the river
I look through the river, I see the sea
I look through the sea, I see the sky.
I am the bard who sings of water
in shriveled seasons.
I say to the oasis: why don't you swell
and swallow the desert?
I tell the desert: why don't you let the rain...?
There is something celestial, I say,
in the moistening lips of pubescent showers

I trace the way of the camel and ponder
the endless patience of the beast's ungainly hump
I ask its long legs, I ask its narrow eyes
I ask the invisible cistern in the kitchen
of its throat;
I ask the Tuareg's wizened beard
footprints of old terrors when salt swapped
hands for pepper, then for teeming lives
from Africa's beleaguered forests.
The Tuareg casts a glance,
and a scroll of chronicles rolls down his silent face;
I chase those chronicles to a distant coast,
the Mediterranean springs a mask
of dated sagas.
I have been through the desert

but there are no sands in the ointment
of my mind

My gold comes from the quarry of the setting sun
my silver from the joyous fin of the sea's abiding tribes
the hen's fresh-laid eggs are the cornea
of my eyes
my body harbors a river in every vein:
the Euphrates, the Ganges, the Mississippi,
the Volga, the Rio, the Niger all seek a shore
in the confluence of my heart;
my fire comes from the parrot's enflamed tail
my camwood from *alokos*[1] red fable;
the sky is my robe
the sky is my robe
my cottonfields are up in the clouds
the sky is my robe

I am what is, is not
the fiction of the fact
the fact of impossible fictions
I am the tail which leads the head
the mouse which worsts the league
of a thousand cats
I am the watering eyes of a savannah
tormented by dubious fires,
I am the mahogany's last curse
on the greedy axe;
I am the grain which blooms the valley
after a handsome shower,
the coquettish lash on the eye of green cliffs.
I am earth's twilight yawn
and also her vigilant dawn:
When I die, Earth will throw open her bosom,
let gravediggers spare their axe.
I am human in every sense
lover of life without regret

ample hips, the bouncing bosom
handsome lips alive with joy
tongues which twist and tangle like exultant vines
a tickle in the armpit, a tickle in the groin
the cool-hot hearth in the valley of the legs

the pestle finds its mortar
the mortar finds its pestle
legs touching legs in a dance beyond the drum
a gentle sigh, a sticky moan
hard and soft is the legend of the flame.
I have seen eyes more eloquent
than a hundred tongues:
the beckoning brow, the warrant of the wink;
I have plucked furtive glances like
a precocious orange,
read a thousand chapters in the book
of the whisper
plunged down, down the depth of the smile

I hold life like a brimming cup
vinegar at times, for the most, wine
with irrepressible spirits.
I drink in song, I drink in dance
I drink, but not too far below the brim:
when I pick my share, I leave the garden behind.

The head leads, the heart follows
The heart leads, the head follows
I think to love, I love to think,
I wear no masks of craven virtues,
for my heart once said to me:
'Be not ashamed of me'

The pine-apple left its honey in my mouth,
the loam-fattened yam put a bounce on my biceps,

tolotolo's[2] thigh is drumstick in my simmering soup;
I share the guinea-corn's glory in the furnace
of the sun,
I trace the way of the grape,
the juicy tang of sleeping cellars,
palm-wine's frothy rage in the divinity of the gourd,
and redolent vows yeasting, yeasting
in the calabash of fleeting seasons.

Let all who sow

share in the harvestfeast
Let all who sow

Share.
The pot which cooks the season's delicacies
must cool its scorched bottom
with the tastiest of royal banquets
Let all who sow
Share.

I hold life like a brimming cup
vinegar at times, for the most, wine
with irrepressible spirits.
I sing a calf to every cow,
to every pig a barn of noisy sows.
I am spirit of the streamside:
my eyebrows are shrubs, incessantly green.

I sing the plenitude of being.

My memories mould the pyramids,
unsilence the Sphinx
rinse pagan hieroglyphs in the Nile
arrest the crack of Pharaoh's whip.
I am a lamp in the tunnel, bold and bright,
beacon in the blindness of the night,

beckoning ships ashore from the wildness
of the sea.
I am the spirit of the making mind
at war with brittle facts
at war with groggy superstitions statued
into giants with iron legs
at war with wills which say yes
to the blood-stained accent of unmanning edicts
at war with spirits afraid of thinking
at war with those who murder the world
with the myth of jealous gods
at war with the hectoring jab, with canons
which whip the world into a hard, invariate mold

at war with former victims of fire who thrive now
through the commerce of the gun
at war with the crocodile who swallows the minnows
at war with all who hasten the day
towards a sudden twilight...
For when life's breathing fingers knock on the door,
I am always there, waiting behind the knob.

'Sing us a happy song, oh poet!
I hear mild protestations from the edge
of the crowd,
Sing us sunny songs, joyous like the showers
of April,
crisp like a piece of *ewura*[3] placed white-hot
on the plate of the smiling child.
Sing to us about rivers, rivers tumbling
down the mountains with a concert
of chorusing fishes.
Sing to us about hills galloping against the sky
like a happy rig of *Udi*[4] horses
Sing to us about egrets echeloned
in the Christmas sky,

a chalky epigram of infinite spaces
Sing to us about the antelope which brightens
the forest with its handsome leaps
Sing to us about paths which meet and part,
part and meet in wandering jungles

Sing to us about the glow-worm's treason
in the darkdom of night

Sing to us about Soyinka, Guillen, Brathwaite,
Neto, Walcott, Ai Qing, Heaney, Mayakovsky,
Okigbo, U Tamsi, Okot p Bitek;
about Neruda, bard of Chile, father of songs,
About Whitman who wrapped the world
in leaves of eloquet grass
Sing to us about Elytis' small world the great,
Vallejo's big-hatted verse,
the laughing lemons of Darwish, victim of a map,

who turned friend of the corn
the day his poems were made of earth
where the feet of the mountain drink the sea;
and Adonis who sailed in the Ark,
reaching liquid skies through the window of prayers

Sing to us about Huidobro,
about the magic lyre of Octavio Paz,
Zapata's arrow in the bow of flying ballads;
about Czeslaw Milosz, 'child of Europe',
walking through the malignant wisdom
of broken cities,
about Amiri Baraka who gathers briefs cinders
for coming thunders,
about Rabindranath Tagore who plants marble lines
on the brow of the Taj Mahal;
about Aime Cesaire whose fear squats
in purple streets, in bardic quest

122

for a tree with a thousand roots

Sing to us about bards, troubadors, griots, towncriers
who joined the earth but left their voices behind.

Sing to us about
the mouth which finds its tongue
the face which finds its nose
the pen which finds its nib
the groom who meets his bride
the slave who breaks his chain...
Sing to us about all this
Sing all this, o poet, and more!'

1. Bird with a deep-red color
2. Turkey
3. Water yam
4. A mountain range in the eastern part of Nigeria

From DIARY OF THE SUN

h
(Goshen, Indiana)

And the sun traces the geo
graphy of History on my glistening brow:
tell-tale creases rippling like water snakes
into the dense foliage of the head

The nose is a heaving island
in the ocean of the face
redolent (still) with vanished whimpers
and the tropical memory of unborn seasons

In the valley between my lips
legends sprout like mushrooms in the first rain,
with domes of fire,
caryatids of eloquent bronze.

There are hungry tremors
in the mountains of the jaw:
a drought-tested spittle slobbers down
the cliff of the palate, the tong

ue is one pink fire in the furnace
of the mouth, slicing through mosaics
of muted murmurs, through dark threnodies
of manacled spurs.

These ebony contours in the deciduous interludes
of evergreen joys, counting pits and peaks
in the solar tempers of undulating masks.
The sun knows the geo-graphy of History

k

Like the soap
which forgives the garment's sin
in the magnanimity of foam,

The sun clears dark shadows
of the terror of the night;
stagnant pools are stirring again

with a fresh census of surging minnows.
The road's muddy kindness
has caked into crimson feast
in the solar kitchen of a centered sky:

toe marks embrace the streets, toe
marks which found their name
in the clayey book of lettering gallops.
For noontide is kiln for supple dreams
reared out of the dew's un

easy womb; running days
have cut their molar: noonwaves
savor the nut of cracking truths...
But heated arguments snake out into rainy concords:
and then another clay, then another dream
like streets fore-giving their shadows.

i

I long for open spaces
After so many seasons in the belly of a myth,
Unlettered by blind legends, lost in
The labyrinthine syntax of unuttered proverbs

I long for open spaces
After the tongue's wordless wanderings
In the cave of the mouth, and lips
Which mourn the scar of keyless locks
I long for open spaces
From edicts which thicken like medieval jungles
And streets which stumble their days

On nights of adamantine orders

I long for open spaces
Like a clearing in the forest
Like a stroll by the sea
Like the bird's blue range in the amplitude of the sky
Like mountains, like rivers,
Like echoes giving back the voice of talkative hills

I long for open spaces
From walls which squeeze the room with concrete claws
And doors which stiffen their hinges
Like sentries from forgotten epochs

I long for open spaces
From smiles which sting like jilted scorpions,
The hidden trap in the track of power hunters
Crimson tantrums in the festival of the knife

From BREAKING WALLS

Breaking walls, walls breaking
in the chilly summon of the dungeon
where silence rides the crest of purple groans
and murmurs pluck their wails from
    the testimony of ruptured spleens

Breaking walls
in the spiked stammer of iron heels polished
to blinding shimmer in a lake of steaming blood,
laced to frenzy by the dripping tendons
    of rifled joints

An iron knuckle unsettles the martial peace of the door
hinges surrender their teeth, and a gecko falls
from the splice of the chaos, flat, medievally dry;
peepholes are blind in one eye; the knob stiffens,
    convulsed beyond recall

Mosquitoes brook the rap without a wink,
serenading indulgently between their meals;
the cockroach preens its pride above the door,
its coat a faithful mirror for blind batons
    aloft on shaven skulls

No sun here: the sky is once upon a season:
a window interrupts the eternity of the wall,
unspaced by iron bars, too high to see the moon;
the sky is a wilderness of barbed wire, of broken bottles
    still sad for their wasted wine.

A guard grabs Detainee 13130013 by the arm,
his skin comes off in scabrous ease;
another prisoner coughs in Cell 770077,

the yard a swarming compost
    of tubercular plague

Music here comes in symphonies of swinging whips
the rasp of iron knuckles on the harp of baring ribs
the tom-tom of the truncheon on the base of stubborn
    spines
sirens of passing powers, rat-a-tat
    of brainless coups

And enter the generals
in crunching boots
and monologues
of talkative triggers

Their whiskers are iron
their lips stone slabs
of crimson edicts;
their gait is gore, stairs

Creak under their breaths;
Sandhurst in their lungs
empire in their dreams
their master's voice so

Loud above their clashing cymbals;
they sentry the exit of wit
shout out the light from
the lamps of venturing feet

Bendless their joints,
kneading ash from breathing clay
plodding across the land, gun—
prints of shells and spent virtue

Fat and rich
they shoot blind guns at tender fortunes,

retire into billions at thirty years,
pampered emperors on purchased thrones

Says Gallileo: the earth I see is round.
And Lorca's head comes smiling in Franco's platter
And Defoe's plague years, with the Crown's slit

in his dissenting ears.
And Brecht hit the waves, Hitler's headhunters
on his epic heels

Says Galileo: the earth I see is round
And Brutus' ballad, and the apartheid dragon
And Soyinka's shuttle in the General's crypt
And Ngugi's travails on the Devil's cross
And Mapanje's chameleons and Band-it gods

Says Galileo: the earth I see is round

Then come jagged visions flat as a foil, saracens of lame
scriptures,
sooth-murderers purple in tooth and claw, peddlers of
expired
faiths, bile merchants, book-burners, maulers of the
breathing
word, night moles, fabricators of monochromatic rainbows,
  scarlet prowlers, knights of the smoking gun

And waiting noons are twilights of pounding hooves, of
crimson dust which falls back to earth, a tribe of sprawling
corpses; and the bridle sews the jaws of the horse: galloping
days are bedlam of neighing tantrums; and iron trots break
the spine of the streets; houses look on with dusty eyes, their
eaves dropping like tired ears; and warriors thunder down
the roads, a cavalry of broken vows.

And streamward maidens lose their flowers, and homeward
hunters forgo their game, and ripening farms forget their
barn, and harvest seasons escape their laughter, and they
swallow the mountain, wash it down with the happiest lake,
then sew up the sky into *boubous* with infinite pockets

And the sky invokes its thunder, and thunder invokes its
lightning: and the *boubou* blooms into a pageant of fire, and
their ashes nurture the waiting loam.

Dare you who will. Dare you, deans of universal nescience.
Dare you conquer truth with bayonets and cannon; your
legs are two, but there are many crossroads on the pilgrimage to enduring wisdom.

Says Galileo: the earth I see is round

So, has Socrates brewed his hemlock? Tell this to the vanish-
ing sun, you who stand between the bee and its hive, the
hen and its lay, the parrot and its tale, the weaverbird and its
nest. Tell it to the bushfowl which turns a night of envy
when the egret drapes the sky in chalky splendor, the
gànyìnganyìn[1] which grudges the pine-apple for its house of
honey, the snail which dreams daggers for the antelope's
savannah heels.

Tell this to the waking sun: this hemlock courts the pride of
the emperor's lips—our dawn has no more nails for the cross
of unsinning Christs.

1. Very sour orange

From MIDLIFE

    Midlife
then in a continent repressed into dire childhood
like *Sogolon's** child, crawling at eighty;
still struggling to count her fingers,
her gray gums toothless with tardy vowels,
her dark silence, her verbless eruptions,
her blanched rainbows, her truncated dreams
and the winds whispering through the trees,
their cheeks whip-marked and utterly sad;
and the storms mangling the dunes,
the Sahara one ocean of weeping sands,
and mountains, pledging ancient peaks,
to indulgent clouds, so scared of roaring plains.
Nights swap garments with days,
the sun staggers into the parlor of an overripe morning,
having slept too long in the chambers
of clever clouds.

The lion has lost its claws
to cheetahs of other forests;
what use, the magnificent mane
of emasculated tantrums

    They who have heads have no caps
    Those who have caps are in need of heads

My continent is a sky ripped apart by clever crows,
awaiting the suturing temper of a new, unfailing Thunder

But tell me, Africa,
Tell me more about this eternal childhood.
I have washed my hands in rivers
of many seasons:
I can now share the feast of ancient wisdoms
I have cut my teeth in forests of sturdy ivory,

*In Sundiata: an Epic of Old Mali by D.T. Niane

131

ripening cornfields drive no fear into my jaws.

Midlife
from now Africa, beholding you, full-length, from shoulders
baked strong by your black sun;
my hands towards the sky, feet towards the sea,
I ask you these with the urgency of a courier
with a live coal in his running palm:

    The skeletal song of Zinjanthropus,
    was it a lie?

    The awesome ruins of Zimbabwe,
    were they fiction?

    The bronze marvels of Benin, of Ife,
    were they a lie?

    Is the Nile really a fickle tear
    down the cheeks of unmemorable sands?

    The geometry of your idoms, the algebra of your
    proverbs,
    were they sad calculations of a pagan mouth?

My question, Africa, is a sickle, seeking
ripening laughters in you deepening sorrows

Giving, giving, always giving,
scorched by the Desert, blanched by the Sea,
bankrupted by the Sun, indebted by the Moon,
robbed of your tongue, bereft of your name

Giving, always giving
ebony springboard for giants of crimson heights
Giving, always giving
my memory is the thrashing majesty of the Congo

its dark, dark waters fleeced by scarlet fingers
its shoals unfinned, its saddled sands
listening earlessly to the mortgaged murmurs
of ravished ores

Giving, always giving
the tall lyric of the forest
the talkative womb of the soil
the mountain's high-shouldered swagger
pawned, then quartered, by purple cabals.
The elephant's ivory is a tale of prowling guns,
the crocodile mourns its hide on the feet
of trampling gods

Giving, always giving
fiery dawns once wore you like a robe, oh Congo,
soft, warm, gracious like the cotton laughter
of Lumumbashi,
the Niger, the Volta, the Benguela
bathed the rippling hem of your luminous garment;
the sky was your loom, April's elephant grass
your needle with a hundred eyes;
your thread was the lofty spool of the eagle,
the chalky string of the egret in the dusty shuttle
of meticulous harmattans

And now noon
with the sun so young in the center of the sky,
that robe is a den of dripping fragments
awaiting the suturing temper of a new, unfailing Thunder

Giving, always giving,
the drums are silent now, their lips bleeding
pale in the slaughtery of iron fingers;
decreed their idioms, their legend roundly mocked
by a cargo of plastic sticks:

Bata[1] coughs out a muffled plaint,
the *Fontonfron*[2] lacks knowing ears for
its pensive proverbs
the *kukunbakus*[3] throb staggers
along the valley, falling back to dust
like a wingless echo.
The wood abhors its skin,
orphaned couriers crouch gracelessly

in the smutty saga of silenced squares,
taunted by the eunuch laughter of swindling winds;
idle legs haul lame curses at the maddening moon
In these seasons of sundering silence
how can the Towncrier hide his gong
in the vanity of seedless clouds?

The night is cold with fright,
white with the simpering laughter of deracinated teeth
a crow describes shrill stunts in the magnitude
of the sky,
one with the night, one with the wordless clatter
of starless regions.
Which firefly will sow a little twinkle
in the infinite furrows of a loamy darkness,
which gallant noon will define itself
by the black plenitude beyond a snoreless slumber?
The night is chill,
a sepia sun gathers strength behind the clouds,
mustering keen faggot for the pneumonia
of the moon.

1. A Nigerian drum
2. A Ghanaian drum
3. An African drum of unknown origin

134

From THREAD IN THE LOOM

I behold

Stubborn roots in league
against the sickle's insistence

The fireflames of mountains
which burn with volcanic splendor

I behold

The unwinding loincloths of men who play god
in temples of wooden angels

The deciduous laughter
of eating chiefs

I behold

The heaviness of the needle,
the weightless truth of fractured visions

The ringing alpha of concluded minds,
the sprouting song of buried virtues

I behold

The plough's glare in the mirror
of the preening soil

seasons stark drunk
on the talent of the grape

I behold

Stars marching back to claim
the patrimony of the night

The revelry of the new moon,
thunder's laughter in the comedy of the sky

I behold

Touching boulders,
The sympathy of stone.

Clouds which full-fill
the promise of rain

From
Waiting
Laughters

*Throughout, to the accompaniment of
drums, horns, and stringed instruments,
if possible the kora or goje. Medley of voices.*

I PLUCK THESE WORDS

I pluck these words from the lips of the wind
Ripe like a pendulous pledge;
Laughter's parable explodes in the groin
Of waking storms
Clamorous with a covenant
of wizened seeds

Tonalities. Redolent tonalities

Of wandering fancies yeasting into mirth,
Yeasting into glee in the crinkled lanes
Of giggling cheeks,
Lingering aroma of pungent chuckles,
The rave of ribs which spell the moments
In latitudes of tender bones

Tonalities. Redolent tonalities

I pluck these murmurs
From the laughter of the wind
The shrub's tangled tale
Plaited tree tops
And palms which drop their nuts

Like talents of golden vows
I listen solemnly to the banter
Of whistling fern
And I reap rustling rows
So fanatic in their pagan promise

Tonalities. Redolent tonalities

And laughing heels so fugitive
In the dust of fleeing truths

Truth of the valley
Truth of the mountain

Truth of the boulder
Truth of the river

Truth of the flame
Truth of the ash

Truth of the sole
Truth of the palm

Truth of the sun
Truth of the moon

Truth of the liar
Truth of the lair

Truth of the castle
Truth of the caste

Truth of the desert
Truth of the rain

Tonalities. Redolent tonalities

The rain. The rain
Truth of the rain's seven ingots
In the womb of the forge
And the seminal smoke which leaps
Above the roof, plodding skylanes
Before taunting thunder's raw temper
To a wild, unbridled deluge

The rain. The rain
The rain is *oníbáńbáńtibá*[1]

The rain is *oníbànbàntibà*
The rain which taunts the roof's dusty laughter
In the comedy of February's unsure showers;
The wind is its wing, the lake
One liquid song in its fluent concert

Tonalities. Redolent tonalities

The wind has left springing laughter
In the loins of bristling deserts;
Sands giggle in grass,
Fallowing pebbles reach for sacks of scrotal pasture

Tonalities. Redolent tonalities

And still fugitive like a fairy,
The wind gallops like a thoroughbred
Dives like a dolphin
Soars into the waiting sky
Like *awodi*[2] with a beak of feathery oracles

Tonalities. Redolent tonalities

And laughing winds
So fugitive in
Our harried seasons
Who can tie
Them down with
                    The rope

Of a single idiom   Who dare?

Tonalities. Redolent tonalities

Blame not, then,
The rapid eloquence of the running vowel
When words turn willing courier

In the courtyard of dodging ears
Can the syllable stall its tale
In impertinences of half-way fancies?

Tonalities. Redolent tonalities

I pluck these words
From the lips of running winds
When earth, yolk-yellow, clamors
For a warrant of wings
Tiptoe on the prudence of an anthill,

My covenant is clay,
Wisdom my silent wheel

Tonalities. Redolent tonalities

1. *Onibanbantiba:* no specific semantic "meaning"; used here as tonal counterpoint.
2. *Awodi:* kite

142

WAIT
ING...

And the hours limp a-
long,
with
band-
ages
of fractured moments

Every minute
heavy like an expectant rock,
the eyes laboring through
a century of winks
   And the horse gallops
   through an eternity of yawns
   through the webbed wandering
   of mangrove patience,
   in the dusty mirror
   which powders the broken mask
   of swindled deserts

The horse gallops
through a street which stretches
like a rubbery code
before slipping a criminal disc
near the sacrum of the moon

Then the road narrows into artery
blossoms into egret dreams
which temper the whitened waiting
of showerless seasons

The road wanders into the street
the street wanders into the road

and road and street mellow into way,
lengthen into vision...

And the hours limp a-
long
longer than an April shower
longer than the cursive laughter of lightning
longer than the silk-cotton tree's mercy
in the loom of naked seasons
longer than the tortuous, broken queues
at the portals of Austerity factories!

Teach us the patience of the sand
which rocks the cradle of the river

Teach us the patience of the branch
which counts the seasons in dappled cropping

Teach us the patience of the rain
which eats the rock in toothless silence

Teach us the patience of the baobab
which tames the rage of orphaning storms

Teach us the patience of the cat
which grooms the thunder of the leaping moment

Teach us, teach us, teach us...

WAITING FOR THE HEIFER

Waiting
   for the heifer which bides its horns
   in the womb of the calf

Waiting
   for the nail which springs an ivory wonder
   in the aprons of the finger

Waiting
   for the tome which split its spine
   in the spotted arena of reading eyes

Waiting
   for the deer which loves its hide
   and hunters who cuddle their flaying guns

Waiting
   for the razor's stubbled glide
   across the firmament of the beard

Waiting
   for fists which find their aim
   and idioms which split their atoms

In 'ploding shadows.

WAITING FOR THE ANXIOUS FUMES

Waiting
    The anxious fumes of the visa awe-ffice
    thick with queries, thick with fear
    and stamps which bite trembling papers
    with purple fangs, and seals pompous
    like a mad phallus

    Narrow, the walls,
    high, imperiously white;
    the hangings stoke wondering dreams
    with their tourist havens;
    the future is one wavering complexion
    of the visaman's edict

Waiting
    in the visahouse is a chronicle of cold complaint:
    the calibrated aircon[1] coughs a chill
    in the sweaty calculations of a room
    aloud with doubt
    Exile, pilgrim, tripsters with feathered heels,
    there is a baggage of patience
    in the missionary temper of wanderlust.

    The visaman, rightly, suited,
    his hair correct, his parting severe
    takes two furtive looks at the crowded hall
    then shuts the window with a cold,
    imperial hiss;

    The crowd's answer is a yawn,
    and a few blank trips to a tired watch.

    Passports are pass ports
    The Atlantic is a wilderness of barbed walls

NIYI OSUNDARE

brooking no windows, its door of deafening steel

The key fell into spaceless water,

once upon a blue dragon,
then vanished, finally, into the shark's
intolerant belly.

Passports are pass ports
Knock still ye who may;
the Atlantic springs a door of deafening steel

And interrogation windows
And reluctant seats
And officers cold and clever

Like inquisitive godlings
And the metallic 'No!'
And rapid ciphers
And repatriated dreams
And wingless fancies
And darkened noons...

Knock still ye who may;
Seconds plod in leaden paces
in crowded visarooms.

1. Aircon: Nigerian abbreviation for air conditioner

WAITING LIKE THE GRASS

Waiting
  like the grass honing every blade
  for the flesh of the dew

Waiting
  like the uncircumcised penis of okro[1]
  peeping out of the prepuce of dawn

Waiting
  like the lip of lettuce, the open palm of
    ṣọkọ̀yọ̀kọtọ̀[2]
  beckoning the sky-bound shower, beckoning

Waiting
  like a raffia brush in the armpit of the valley,
  iron straws on hips of dancing groves

Waiting
  like the beard for its chin, the knee for its cap
  the night for its day, the prayer for its amen

Waiting
  like the forest for the umbrella of its mushroom
  like the earth for the husband of its sky

Waiting
  like the tyrant for his noose.

---

1. *okro:* vegetable with long green pods; sometimes called okra
2. *Ṣọkọ̀yọ̀kọtọ̀:* make-the-husband-robust; a favorite Nigerian
  vegetable

WINNOWING SEASON:
WE-KNOWING-SEASON

Winnowing season: we-knowing-season
The chaff know their hell,
grains thresh a handsome pilgrimage
to the Jerusalem of the jaw;
and pumpkins unfold yellow peril
in the ripening ridges of compassionate suns

Winnowing season: we-knowing-season

"I am Croesus," quoth he,
waiting
his breath a gail of gold,
his swagger varnished silver of a low intemperate sky

His head asks his crown
for a humble place in its gilded castle;
the crown pulls the head by its servile hair,
then leaves it hanging like an orphaned burden

Beyond Reason, beyond Necessity
beyond Distribution which tames the Excess
of uneven mountains
beyond Virtue, beyond Need
beyond Truth which straightens the serpent
of stammering jungles
Croesus heaves a glittering crown on his head,
his neck shortening like a senile cricket's

Beyond Reason, beyond Necessity
in the orgy of crimson claws
which darken the rainbow of striving ribs
in the belly of the goblet where murdered grapes

sip their scarlet wails,
the moon, the moon, is up;
the scepter barks its canine edict

castles crash, mortally tired of their medieval legs

waters breaking, waters breaking
royal fishes smell purple twilight
in the cemetery of baking sands

WAITING LIKE THE BASTILLE

Waiting
   like the Bastille, for the screaming stones
   of turbulent streets;
   their bread is stone
   their dessert garnished sand from the kitchen
   of hearthless seasons
   And when the humble axe finally heeds its noble
     task,
   the head descends, lumpen dust in its royal mouth

Behold the wonder;
the crown is only a cap!

     Orogododo Orogodo
     Orogododo Orogodo
     Ọba ba ti bẹyi
     Omod Orogododo o o o o[1]

     The king's brave legs are bone and flesh
     Bone and flesh, bone and flesh
     The king's brave legs are bone and flesh
     The castle is a house of mortar and stone
     Mortar and stone, mortar and stone
     A chair is wood which becomes a throne

     And Croesus builds a castle of strident stone.
     Oh teach us the patience of the Rain
     which eats the rock in toothless silence

1. *Orogododo Orogodo*
   A king who dances with a dizzy swing
   Orogodo straight he goes

   (*Orogodo* in Ikere mythology is a remote place of banishment for dishon
orable rulers)

WAITING ON THE STAIRS OF THE MOON

Waiting
   on the stairs of the moon
   creaking up and down
   the milkyways of fastidious comets
   bled into speed, plucked off the vortex
   of falling flares
   my foot knows the timbre of fiery skies
   where songs still dripping
   with the sap of the wind
   dry their limbs in furnaces
   of baking proverbs

   My song is space
   beyond wails, beyond walls
   beyond insular hieroglyphs
   which crave the crest
   of printed waves.

MY SONG IS THE EVEN RIB

My song is the even rib
in the feather of the soaring bird
the pungent salt and smell of earth
where seeds rot for roots to rise

My song is the root
touching other roots
in a covenant below the crust
beyond the roving camera of the eye

My song is the embryo of day
in the globule of the rising dew;
a vow which earths the Word
in regions of answerable rains

My song is *ògbìgbòtirigbò*[1]
waiting on the stairs of the moon
garnering lights, garnering shadows,
waiting

1. *Ògbìgbòtirigbò*. a bird which flies high in the sky

THE INNOCENCE OF THE NIGER

The innocence of the Niger
waiting, waiting
fourhundredseasons
for the proof of the prow
waiting
for the irreverent probing of pale paddles
waiting
for the dispossessing twang of alien accents
    waiting
for scrolls of serfdom, hieroglyphs of calculated
    treacheries
waiting
withoutafacewithoutanamewithoutafacewithouta-
waiting
for the Atlantic which drains the mountains with
practiced venom
waiting
for a history which snails towards the coast,
a delta of meandering dreams
waiting
for the bubbles of Bussa
where rock riles river and a conquering boat
fathoms the sand in a tumble of misty furies
waiting
the Nile knows the Limpopo lingers,
the Kilimanjaro preserves the lore in its icy memory
waiting
    But for how long can the hen wait
    Whose lay is forage for galloping wolves?

Ask Sharpeville
ask Langa
ask Soweto

Where green graves cluster like question marks

Ask Steve
ask Walter
ask Nelson

who seed waiting moments with sinews of fleeting
    seasons

Ask
    the metaphor of our strength

Ask
    the strength of our metaphor

Ask
    the breaking, broken stones of Robbing Island
    where the ocean's water is sulphur
    where aching walls harbor a dragon
    in every crack

Ask
    the bleeding anthem on the lips of wounded kraals

Ask
    the dappled darings on billowing banners

Dappled
    like the grave where Sankara lies, a waiting eagle,
    Dappled
    like the windward dream of Bishop

Dappled
    like the seeing History of Rodney

Ask:
    the stone under Nelson's hammer is bread

river with faithful wings
wind the jasmine in its breath;

Ask
the stone is an ocean

which cannot count its shoal of eyes

Waiting
for the kaffir buried four hundred days a year
in orphaning pits
for the Boer trapped by the diamond dazzle
of unanswerable plunderings

Time ambles in diverse paces...

WAITING, STILL WAITING

Waiting,
still waiting,
like the strident summon of hasty edicts,
bellowed by the smoking lips of vulgar guns,
signed in blood, unleashed in the crimson spine
of trembling streets

And the winds return,
laden with adamantine thou-shalt-nots
of green gods;
a jointless Fear goosesteps the compound of our minds
with epaulettes of night, belts of fuming cobras;
purple swaggers manacle our days
and trees swap their fruits for stony orders

    These are seasons of barking guns
    These are seasons of barking guns;
    They whose ears are close to the earth
    Let them take cover in the bunker of their wits

The lion grows iron-maned and bans the flock
The crocodile turns stone-jawed and bans the shoals

The cloud grows cotton-headed and bans the rain
The valley turns tunnel-hearted and bans the river

The sky grows swollen-headed and bans the sun
The sea turns beady-eyed and bans its salt
The shogun grows cannon-drunk and bans himself
But are these the messiahs
who came four seasons ago
with joyful drums and retinues of chanted pledges?
Where now the aura,
where, the anointed covenant of eloquent knights?

*   *   *

And bellowed the shogun
with a swaggering viper in his armpit,
a raging geyser in his regimented nose
Bellowed the shogun
with a dusky grain around his lips:

| I proscribe | the snail |
| I proscribe | the shell |

| I proscribe | the frog |
| I proscribe | the tadpole |

| I proscribe | the sea |
| I proscribe | the sky |

| I proscribe | the sun |
| I proscribe | the moon |

| I proscribe | the tale |
| I proscribe | the TRUTH |

| I proscribe | HISTORY! |

* * *

The bison who thinks he is the king of the wild
    let him remember raging elephants
        with legs of mortar

The hillock which thinks it is the frontier of heights
    let it remember the Kilimanjaro so hot
        with a peak of simmering snow

The streamlet which thinks it is the Zambesi of the lore

let it remember the sea which merges earth
    and sky in realms of misty blue

The prophet who thinks he has conquered tomorrow
    let him mount galloping mountains and marvel
        dodging canters of the horse of time

The shogun who says he is an awesome god
    let him take note of burning statues
        and streets wild with vengeful spears...

*   *   *

And waiting,
still waiting,
like the mouth for its fiery tongue.

WAITING LIKE THE POTHOLE

Waiting
   like the pothole for its po(r)tion of blood

   Like the smart General for his umpteenth million

   like idle bugs for their nightly feast

   like the prattling tongues of parliaments of ruse

   like Blaise for a trusting Thomas

   like Imelda for her shoes.

WAITING LIKE A HYENA

Waiting
    like a hyena
    for the anniversary of its pounce;
    waiting
    like an African despot
    for the seventieth year of his rule.

OKEREBU KEREBU

Okerebu kerebu
Kerebu kerebu

And the snake says to the toad;
"I have not had a meal
For a good one week;
And my stomach yearns
For your juicy meat"

"Suppose I turn into a mountain?
Asks the toad,

"I will level you in the valley
Of my belly"

"Suppose I turn into a river?

"You will flow easily through
The channels of my mouth"

"Suppose I become one
Of your favorable children?"

"I will eat you
With all the motherly love
In this world"

The toad then turns into a rock
And the snake swallows it
With delicious dispatch

Ah! *aramonda*[1]
The mouth has swallowed something
Too hard for the mill of the stomach

162

Okerebu kerebu
kerebu kerebu

Our tale is a bride
Waiting

For the nimble fancy of the grooming ear.

1. *Aramonda* wonder of wonders

WHOEVER HASN'T KISSED

Whoever hasn't kissed the sticky lips
of an envelope
licked the glossy spine of a stamp,
lacing pigeon winds with syllables
of feathered breaths

Whoever hasn't fondled the legend of the grape
teased the mammary temper of the joyous pawpaw
incited humble carrots to riot,
swollen with the pink bluff
of February's relentless sun

Whoever hasn't trampled the wound of the road
touched sour streets on their bruised elbow
mopped the copper sore of August

Whoever hasn't touched the armpit of the rock
watched care-less boulders tremble
with potent laughter
savored the jubilant tears of lilting lava

Whoever hasn't seen a caravan of Ways
racing after their dashing Means…

Whoever hasn't,

is still waiting.

WAITING LIKE THE ETERNAL WISDOM

Waiting
like the eternal wisdom of
Mosáféjó[1]
who gave one daughter
in marriage to six suitors

1. *Mosáféjó*. I-am-averse-to-litigations

SOWING

And when a long-awaited shower
has rid earth's brow
of the debris of sweltering seasons

When heavy clouds have known
their labor, and a steel-handed sun
midwives the mists

in noons of convectional brewings,
rivers learn once more
their liquid lessons, the valley so

   quick with veins of fresh tiding

When a long-awaited shower
has softened the pilgrimage of the dibble,
corn-grains sing their way to germinal roots

of lying ridges. Seedlings dream truant tendrils
in the moistening bed of unpunctual heaps;
the tuber is one patience away,

climbing through stakes
through pinna-leafed groves
through vines which twine the moons

   like wayward pythons

Bent now
the farmer's back;
the hoe's edict chills the spine

of sowing seasons. And the sweat
which rivers down the mountain of the brow,

finds gathering basin at the root of coming harvests

Oh seminal seasons
oh moons of sporing shadows;
laughing barns are just a tear away

and the plenitude which threshes the throes of
                    ripening valleys

WAITING...GRANT US

Waiting
still waiting

Grant us

the fortitude of the lamb which lames the lion-
without inheriting its claws

the daring of the egg which hardens its temple
in a golgotha of breaking shells

the valor of the abyss which hurls its crest
above the conspiracy of severe mountains

the wisdom of seasons which see
the hidden dagger in a plumage of smiles

Grant us

the depth of the sky, height of the sea
fancies which flesh the bones of grating facts

moons which dwell the sky of every brow
on nights when love's labor is never lost.

From
Moonsongs

PHASE I
(To the accompaniment of lively woro drumming, the following song, in call-and-response)

> *Peree o pere yoju lorun*
> *Agbamurere*

> *Peree o pere yoju lorun*
> *Agbamurere*

> *Aseseyo osu o dabi ẹgbin*
> *Agbamurere*

> *Ka koṣu kobi ka lọ mu ṣaya*
> *Agbamurere*

> *Ka to debẹ o ti bọjọlọ*
> *Agbamurere*

> *Kiriji kiriji pepelupe*
> *Agbamurere*[1]

Spread the sky like a generous mat
Tell dozing rivers to stir their tongues
Unhinge the hills
Unwind the winds
The moon and I will sing tonight

Kiriji kiriji pepelupe...

Oh moon, matron, master, eternal maiden.
The bounce of your bosom
The miracle of your cheeks
Your smile which ripens the forests

Your frown which wrinkles the dusk
The youth of your age

The age of your youth
All, all await
The echoing thunder of my riddling chants

Kiriji kiriji kiriji pepelupe...

Let the cricket slit night's silence
With the scalpel of its throat
Let nightbirds coo and cuddle
In the swinging Eden of their nests;
But when dawn finally climbs down
Through the leering rafters,
I will be a promise
Eternal like your seasonless sky

Kiriji kiriji pepelupe...

And the moon masters the stars
Masters the sea
Sharpens every tip of its tidal teeth
Rattles every grain of its salty roost
Probes every drop of its diurnal blue
Ah! there are latitudes of sweat
On the brow of the sea;
A tropical truth taunts the waves
Surging beachwards like an armada
Of foaming sharks

Kiriji kiriji pepelupe...

Bell-ringers, the shells shout time's segments
In the dormitory of dodging depths
Heard, not hearing,
Kneaded into millennial reefs and rocks
By the distant fingers of clever water
The penguin smells the moon
In the graying hem of its clumsy coat,

The beaches chew their sands
With the gritty vigor of rootless teeth

Kiriji kiriji pepelupe...

New-sprung from the tabernacle of iron clouds,
The moon is a wandering sickle

Of gathering vows
With a dialect of whispers, covenant of simmering sighs:

The gallant plucks her like a fairy petal
On nights when the lanes are low
And flaming breaths tickle the ears of patient walls,
When moonmaids bathe lunar cycles in the blue mercy
Of scarlet waters
Their heads wavelocks of plaited bubbles;
Their wardrobe is mist,
Their sandals beadwork of fiery scales

Kiriji kiriji pepelupe...

Fiery scales, fiery scales
So eloquent in the manhood of the sun

Oh sea
        season...
                        seasun...

The sun which blues the sea,
Which tones its flesh,
Before chasing twilight's orange
To the fringes of distant depths

Kiriji kiriji pepelupe...

Beyond the palms, beyond the paddles

Beyond shimmering limits
Where the sea hugs the sky with a liquid passion,
The moon reads sunsteps in the alphabet
Of protean sands,
The moon heals the scars of wounded winds

Kiriji kiriji pepellupe...

Spread the sky
Unwind the wind

Let moonmares rein in the infinity
Of galloping hours.

Spread the sky
Unwind the wind
Let moommares shape the amplitude
Of sundry strivings

Peree o pere yoju lorun
Agbamurere...

1. Fresh, fresh does the moon appear in the sky
    Agbamurere
   New moon is beautiful like a fairy
    Agbamurere
   Bring yams, bring kolanuts, let's go and marry her
    Agbamurere
   Before we get up there she has gone with Time
    Agbamurere

174

PHASE II

The moon is a mask dancing
          mask dancing
          mask dancing

The moon is a mask dancing

And in the milky grove
between the cloudmountains
the moon's tropical eyes
are chameleons of silver forests

The moon is a mask dancing

Her lips coiled
like corridors of a thousand snakes
breathing hot, breathing cold
lilting labial lyrics of tangled nights
Oh moon, mother me in the surging valley
of your knowing bosom:
there are clanging amours
in the aprons of the forests,
twilight clears a throat of bleeding spears,
     let dawn clip the tongue of murdering drums
     let dawn clip the tongue of murdering drums

The moon is a mask dancing

And in the tempered peace which rustles
the dew of nodding forests,
in the silence which fore-goes
the gallop of fertile thunders
let me see your voice
so lithe, so light, like eggs of starsparrows
     I will not let fall the eggs

I will not let the eggs fall

The moon is a mask dancing

PHASE III

I must be given words to refashion futures like a healer's hand

—Edward Kamau Brathwaite

We called the statue
To a talking feast
Before knowing the chisel
Never left a tongue in its rigid mouth...

    From the silence of the seasons
    From the hush which murdered the wind
    With thunder's sword
    We borrow the restless throat of *adoko*[1]
    We borrow the permanent query
    On the parrot's beclamored beak

From the vowel of the river
From the consonant of striving valleys
We name the moon, we name the sun
We pledge a fluent chatter to the stammering sea

From seasons which pass but never part
I borrow moonbeans to shape the wind.

---

1. *adoko:* a bird noted for incessant songs

PHASE V

Frantic as a prentice poet
the young moon unfolds,
a wickless lamp
in the silence of lingering nights

trees preen their tops
walls unplug their ears
and hills advance,
minding every crater
on memory's road

moonrays have flared into song
the ballad sizzles in the chimney
of crooning noses;
stars red up the sky
with echoes of silver breaths

can it smell the echo, can it see the chant
a sky whose ears are sealed
by the wax of waning moons?

can it hear
when syllables thrum angry triggers
and consonants fall from heaven
like a hail of vengeful scorpions?

like a troubadour
the moon unfolds her songs
by dusty roadsides of the sky;
the moon unfolds her songs
nomadic like a restless truth

PHASE VI

Night after night
the wind spreads out the sky

And the moon, too busy to sleep,
snatches fleeting dreams in tunnels
of nodding clouds,
swaying so solemnly to the summon
            of the drum
                    of the drum
so loud now with the membrane of the sun

And with its rhythm of rocks
memory of meadows
hieroglyph of hills
with its ding-dong of dawn-and-dusk
the moon lilts and laughs,
a millennial tear standing hot
in the amplitude of its eye

The tear bursts into brook
ripens into river
then gallops like a liquid mare
towards the sea

All at dawn
when the moon is a seasoned navel
in the stomach of the sky.

PHASE X

Tell me, moon,
Where are your wrecks
Where are your wrinkles
Where, the creases left
On your wondrous robe
By the crow-foot fury
Of the wandering wind?

The tendril plies the seasons
And reaps the sponge,
The river's hot-browed swagger
In the empire of the mountain
Softens so slowly into the mellow commonwealth
Of the spreading coast;
The universe sows its minutes, reaps its hours:
Grey strands run their course on the bristling asphalt
Of cruising dreams.

Ashes are the echo of fire
The nose is the memory of the face
The drum is an open hint of a hide
That loved its flesh

The universe sows its minutes, reaps its hours.

And in those moments of joyous ripening
When green turns gold and gold melts
Into phantoms of wizened silver
Ticking mountains fine-ally strike their hour
And the world quakes with streaks of solar depths
Beyond the wilderness of stone
Beyond valleys of suffocating veils
Beyond Wednesdays of unpenitent ash
A Monday flings open the door of the week,

A pliant clay in its waking hand:
Supple moments, of supple moments!
And brittle breaths unchain the dance

And ample hands unhush the drum
Not even the salt of the sea, so bitter
With foams of epileptic scars
Not even the deciduous hustle of declining herbs
Can gray this dappled dream
So gently planted in the temple of our sleep
The universe which sows its minutes
Will reap its hours

PHASE XII
(for Joan Rayfield, tenderer of fertile cultures)

Moonfire too is deciduous;
its conifers weep their leaves
like yellow tears;

And in the dappled darings
of autumn
when yearning winds press lyrical lips
on the apple's demurring bosom,
skyfields are sweaty tracks
for the garnerer's unwavering feet

There is a golden chatter
in the bowers of busy barns
the air leans low with the fragrance
of active ripening;
moonchildren plod skyways
with baskets of mellowed vows
and the stars are heavy pods
of jolly juice

And the seasons which stirred the sod
which hoed the humus
when moonfields were green elves
sprouting from a vibrant wilderness of lunar pores;
those seasons, where are they now,
this moment of delicious shadows?

*Işę losupa nse lalede orun, lalede orun
Işę losupa nse...*[1]

But good old Armstrong
in his weightless walk,
did he trample moonharvests

in the science of green visions?

1. Busy is the moon in the compound of the sky
   Busy is the moon

PHASE XVI

Now I know why the caged bird sings
Why the caged bird sings
Why the caged bird sings
Now I know why the caged bird sings
When the Moon is a knot of strings

The slope of night finally loiters
through the convex cornea of the sky;
and silence rakes up the streets
with epaulettes of terror

Now I know why the caged bird sings

A kiwi-ed boot traps a star
in a regimented shimmer
the skybird flips and flaps
as a cagey night now turns
a galaxy of sweating feathers

Now I know why the caged bird sings

Why the caged bird sings
Why the caged bird sings
Why the caged bird chants every note
on the saddle of crawling hours
when swagger sticks twine into
blustering vipers in the trembling squares
of our gathering fears
patriarchs who plough the word
are snake-charmers now
in the streetcorner of our dreams

Now I know why the caged bird sings

The General missiles a swagger

and a nest of edicts jets out
of his adamantine mouth...

The general is up, up, up
The general is up
There is a beltful of scars
In the furrows of our sweating backs

Now I know why the caged bird sings

Night
when minutes goose-step
in barracks of golden eggs,
the barrel of the gun ever so smooth
with crudes of petroleum rackets

Now I know why the caged bird sings

Why the caged bird sings
Why the caged bird sings
The night ticks on like a giant clock;
and the young moon eyes its infant watch:
Dawn will not be long
Dawn will not be long
Then shall we all know

Why the caged bird sings.

PHASE XVII

The lion borrows its name
from the eloquence of its mane;
the forest's *oriki*[1]
is the green syllable
of towering trees.

And what dumb gold
when drought has mined the leaves
and the birds, voiceless vagrants,
drift, drift, north with their baggage of songs?

The world is a mask dancing
             mask dancing
             mask dancing
Every agile sole knows the sizzling symphony
of the winged dust.

There is a fleeting flock
in the pasture of the moon:
the shepherd senses his twilight
in the static mirror of the eye of the sheep

The rain fell in June
and December licked it brown
with its feline tongue:
they who marvel the sinews of our dust
let them ask what happened to the offsprings
of our yester-showers

The rain is going going going
like a long-besotted bride
But if the sun drags the river
into its scorching harem,
can it lift the sands
from the armpit of earth?

The world is a mask dancing

1. *oriki*. a praisename

186

PHASE XIX

A madding moon
has sold the stars
sold the rocks
there is a bickering banter

in the budget of the sky.
The moon plundered the gold
drained the diamonds
and bartered its silvery ore

to the merchants of night
whose claws are cold
whose teeth are crowded tusks
of the ivory of our dreams

The moon has felled the forests
laundered the lakes
harassed the hills:
a yellowing chill stalks

the steps of lunar magnates.
The moon borrows a bullion from Mars
pawns hapless moonchildren to Jupiter;
and when skysages challenge

the dimness of the deeds
the moon pleads its sword,
pleads the bayonet tongue
of its eager guns
Now the moon has crowned our silence
gripped our songs
laid a frenzied ambush
for the syllable of our sooth
A madding moon

has sold the stars...
And when a wounded thunder
seeks the sanctity of the skies

Ah! The moon, the moon
will be one rotting pumpkin
in the fringes
of a smoking dawn.

PHASE XXII

Ikoyi[1]

> The moon here
> is a laundered lawn
> its grass the softness of infant fluff;
> silence grazes like a joyous lamb,
> doors romp on lazy hinges
> the ceiling is a sky
> weighted down by chandeliers
> of pampered stars

Ajegunle[2]

> here the moon
> is a jungle,
> sad like a forgotten beard
> with tensioned climbers
> and undergrowths of cancerous fury:
> cobras of anger spit in every brook
> and nights are one long prowl
> of swindled leopards

The moon is a mask dancing...

1. & 2. *Ikoya* and *Ajegunle* are areas in Lagos

PHASE XXIV

think of our eyes
sharing one sky
—Joseph Bruchac: *'Awatawesu'*

Gather your hems now
Unfurl your shadows
Tell your fairy feet the road is waiting
Time for that last dance across
The threshold of the swaying sky

    Softly softly
    Softly sways the masquerade of the seasons

Unflinching brow, you who once lit up
The temple of the sky,
Golden pumpkin now in the furnace of dawn,
You have kindled the comb of the cock
Lending rising eaves their misty trumpet

    Softly softly
    Softly sways the masquerade of the seasons

Across silver continents
Across oceans of rippling dust
Beyond deciduous discs of winking groves
Beyond tall chronicles of whispering depths
Across silence, beyond the superstition of the sea

    Softly softly
    Softly sways the masquerade of the seasons

Across the gripping muse-ic of the waking grass
In the throbbing cadence of busy nests
From the ancient chamber of patient drums

Songs ripen the fetus of the day

A misty rhapsody clears the throat of yawning dawns

    Softly softly
    Softly sways the masquerade of the seasons

The palm tenderly pledges its wine
To the parting queen,
The lake throws up its favorite fish
The hill gently yields its eloquent echo
Trees wave their leaves like bewitching fans

    Softly softly
    Softly sways the masquerade of the seasons

Behold the blue distance of prancing mountains
Behold the mellow magic of romping clouds
Behold the fairy laughter of homing maidens
With baskets of stars, garlands of crispy suns
Behold the amplitude which teases the edge of beaming
skies

    Softly softly
    Softly sways the masquerade of the seasons

Quiet now the fancy of the forge
Dew-drenched, the tongue of seminal fires
Quiet now the dialect of the adze
Mist-mobbed, the prattle of the hoe
Quiet, quiet the pod of stirring seeds

    Softly softly
    Softly sways the masquerade of the seasons.

MONDAY MORNING
(at Ibadan University)

staccato syntax
of metalled heels
confounding clamor
of sartorial colors
and
per..fumes loud-
er than waterfalls

Oh what frantic resurrection
after the festive golgotha
of passionate saturdays!
What painless awakening
after the red-light gethsemane
of crisbo gardens[1]

and then
the dozing galilee
of lecture rooms
the seraphic snore
in library carrels...

Monday morning
week's January
when doors slammed
on stubborn sins
await the sledge hammer
of dire fridays

1. *Crisbo Gardens* is a popular nightclub in Ibadan

NOONVIEW

the laughing sun
   unties

the knot of quibbling birds
in their feathery parliament
below the trees...

   A fiery edict has sealed
   the larynx of the lyre
   And the forest leaps into green lores
   of song and rage:
   "Truth banners, truth banners,
   should they ever bear
   the banner of truth?"

*   *   *

Ruthless as a jealous artist
a raging wind wrinkles up
the garment of the forest
   every line a furrow
   on a grudging brow,
   every vein a streak
   of sneaky oaths

*   *   *

...and memory which breaks
the teeth of the grave...
   what happens to the snail
   which left its shell
   in the lengthy crevice of an absent rock?
   what hint, the mouth
   which lost its tongue

in the labyrinth of the throat?

Ah! The giant stands in the riddling sun
but cannot see his musing shadow

Cannot see his shadow
cannot see his shadow
rippling like a molten puzzle
in the gray truth of lengthening dusks

*   *   *

And boasts the drunken tyrant:
"My chains are iron
My walls are stone
My breath is the raging fire
Of skydragons..."

But death came,
not like a pounding giant
with legs of mortar,
not like a swaggering mountain
with a crown of dizzy clouds.
Death came
in the sneaky column
of meticulous rains,
in the yellow whisper
of the wind

Death came
in the stammering murmur of thunder

And...

SHADOWS OF TIME[1]
(Anniversary of a future remembered)

The clouds drift by,
nimble puppies with eyes of marble:
the sun dissolves in the hands of journeying winds
then hardens into balls of ticking stone

    I heard moonsteps in the corridors of seasons
    The sky is aflame with dusts of hurrying dials

Night melts into day melts into night
and the sun, caught between two twilights,
essays moving shadows of dew and dawn;
beyond rigid longitudes of uneven chimes
beyond alien meridians of patterned crossings
the sun bares its clocky face:
its seconds of stars, its speedy hands
playing minute pranks with pendulums of History

    I heard moonsteps in the corridors of seasons
    The sky is aflame with dusts of hurrying dials

For Time, too, has its latitudes:
the dripping rags of tumbling comets,
the lateral slit of the prompting drum
the restless spring of the heels of the egret
cruising home to hearths of chalky depths.
Ah! Time's latitude
is the petulant green of the tendril
the golden prepuce of the pawpaw
the crimson song of the bleeding grave

    I heard moonsteps in the corridors of seasons
    The sky is aflame with dusts of hurrying dials

Memory's minion all:
trees reckoning rings on the ripening finger
of mating forests,
the insolent gray in the jungle of the sage's beard,

the *okro*[2] which, counting days, springs steel fibers
against the conquering knife,
those frantic dreams left in pawprints
of leonine mountains, awaiting
the leveling showers of angry clouds

    I heard moonsteps in the corridors of seasons
    The sky is aflame with dusts of hurrying dials

The harmattan looks back
   and sees the rain
the rain looks forward
   and smells the egret
Life's tides crash and crest
in the oceans of our growing eyes,
fling their fangs at the banks of our dodging dreams,
then slither seawards, a rippling python.
The tides, those tides, will come again
when the moon of our noon is crescent
above the roofs
they will come again
when the sun of our night
is hearth for our tropical strivings

    I heard moonsteps in the corridors of seasons
    The sky is aflame with dusts of hurrying dials

Time's door leans
on hinges of uncertain shores,
oiled by sooth,
dimpled by knuckles
of accumulated visions.

Keyholes here are dioramas
of purple thrones
guessed now from rusty maces
and excavated grandeurs of gray edicts.

Time
Time never runs its race

Like a straight, uncluttered road

Ah Time never does
In Time's street are treacherous bows
And friendly bends,
Crucibles of 'Crucify him!',
Alleys of hallelujahs;
The chameleon joins eyes
With owls of luminous nights
But the forest still cannot see the bird
On tomorrow's tree...

Time is the robe
Time is the wardrobe
Time is the needle's intricate pattern
In the labyrinth of the garment
Time is the lingering aroma
Of a long forgotten dish

Time the seasons
Season the times;
The forest sprouts, blooms
And rots into seed
The seed mothers the mountain
The mountain mothers the river
And the river springs green flowers
In Edens of unsinning apples
    I heard moonsteps in the corridors of seasons
    The sky is aflame with dusts of hurrying dials

Deciduous,
then, the smile of the moon
deciduous
the leafy fire on the brows of the sun
Time masters our steps like a general
with a thousand stars,
drills our manifold musings like a grindstone
with a thousand teeth;
we fret, we fight, we pacify mortality

with busts of stone,
monuments of loudest steel;

but the rains capture rusty chinks
in the shield of steel
storms soften stony prides into
flakes of weathered dust;
wrinkles buried so fashionably by
centuries of rosy talcum
embarrass the face after one wink
of hasty sweating...But

Evergreen,
Time lives in other dreams,
evergreen:
the song of the busy adze
the breath of the forge
the unfettering energy of the word,
minds touching minds touching matter

a strand of gray left in the twilight wind,
a favorite dish, a characteristic smile,
the world catches the fragrance
of our flowering visions
blooming petals of everlasting gardens

Evergreen
their breaths, who stoke the flames
of our flickering fancies

Evergreen
their winds, who lace silent echoes
with rattles of fertile thunders

Evergreen
    ever green

    I heard moonsteps in the corridors of seasons
    The sky is aflame with dusts of hurrying dials

1. Dedicated to the 70th anniversary of *West Africa*, the London-based
   news magazine in which the poem also made its first appearance.
2. *okro.* a vegetble; sometimes called okra.

From
The Eye
of the Earth

EARTH

Temporary basement
and lasting roof

first clayey coyness
and last alluvial joy

breadbasket
and compost bed

rocks and rivers
muds and mountains

silence of the twilight sea
echoes of the noonsome tide

milk of mellowing moon
fire of tropical hearth

spouse of the roving sky
virgin of a thousand offsprings

Ògéérẹ́ amọ́kọ́yerí[1]

---

1. *Ògéérẹ́ amọ́kọ́yerí.* the one that shaves his head with the hoe.

From FOREST ECHOES
(with flute and heavy drums)

A green desire, perfumed memories
a leafy longing lure my wanderer feet
to this forest of a thousand wonders.
A green desire for this petalled umbrella
of simple stars and compound suns.
Suddenly, so soberly suddenly,
the sky is tree-high
and the horizon dips into an inky grove
like a masquerade scribbling loric fear
in the lines of festival streets.

    The rains have kept their time this year
    (Earth has (finally) won the love of the sky)
    Trees bob with barkward sap
    and leaves grab a deepening green
    from the scanty sun.

Bouncing boughs interlock overhead
like wrist wrestlers straining muscularly
on a canvas of leaves wounded
by the fists of time
I tread, soft-soled, the compost carpet
of darkling jungles
my nose one charmed universe
of budding herbs and ripening roots
I tread the compost carpet of darkling forests
where terror grows on trembling leaves
natured by lore
nurtured by fairy truths

Here, under this awning, ageless,
the clock, unhanded, falls
in the deep belly of woods

its memory ticking songfully
in *elulu's*[1] sleepless throat
Mauled the minutes, harried the hours;

taunted is time whose needle's eye
gates our comings and goings

time which wombed the moon
to bear the sun,
the hole in the ragged wardrobe
the gap in the ageing teeth
the bud on the ripening tree
Oh time,
coffin behind the cot.

And every toemark on the footpath
every fingerprint on every bark
the ropy climbers flung breathlessly
from tree to tree
the haunting sound and silence
of this sweet and sour forest
dig deep channels to the sea of memory.
And the outcome:
will it be flow or flood...

---

1. *elulu.* Bird which sings at regular times of the day; also called the time-keeper bird.

THE ROCKS ROSE TO MEET ME

I
(To be chanted with agba drum throbbing in the background)

The rocks rose to meet me
like passionate lovers on a long-awaited tryst.
The rocks rose to meet me
their peaks cradled in ageless mists.
Olosunta[1] spoke first
the eloquent one
whose mouth is the talking house of ivory
Olosunta spoke first
the lofty one whose eyes are
balls of the winking sun
Olosunta spoke first
the riddling one whose belly is wrestling ground
for god and gold.

"You have been long, very long, and far,"
said he, his tongue one flaming flash
of unburnable gnomes
"Unwearying wayfarer,
your feet wear the mud of distant waters
your hems gather the bur
of fartherest forests;
I can see the westmost sun
in the mirror of your wandering eyes."
So saying, he smiled
the trees swaying their leafy heads
in the choreography of his moving lips
so saying, the sun lifted the wrinkle of clouds
from the face of a frowning sky.

Olosunta spoke first
the elephant hand which hits the haughty man in the
head

and his testicles leak to the wondering earth
like overripe *oro* fruits in a thunderstorm
Olosunta spoke

his belly still battle ground of god and gold.
The god I have killed
since wisdom's straightening sun
licked clean the infant dew of fancy
The gold let us dig,
not for the gilded craniums
of hollow chieftains
(time's undying sword awaits their necks
who deem this earth their sprawling throne).
With the gold let us turn hovels into havens
paupers into people (not princes)
so hamlets may hear
the tidings of towns
so the world may sprout a hand
of equal fingers.

Yield your gold, lofty one.
But how dig the gold
without breaking the rock?

II

Òròólè¹ came next
his ancient voice tremulous
in the morning air
(harmattans here whip with the flaying fury
of a slavemaster,
but how can we banish them
without a season of unripened peas?)

Pyramid of the brood,
you who rob your head to pay your foot:
for earth is where we stand

earth is where we strive,
and what greater vantage to a wrestling rock
than a platform of a thousand feet?

Behold, cornfields flourish around your foot
elephant grass fallows the land
for unborn harvests.

Swell the grain
with living water from your rocky arteries,
fatten the tuber,
so the hoe does not scoop a sterile clod
so the dibble does not drill a defeaned dross.
Pyramid of the brood
whose unclosing eyes witness
every stroke and every dot at *Àmòyè*.[2]
You who loomed so fearsomely close
in the harmattan dawns of our learning days
before withdrawing into stony distance
with the noonward sun.

III

The rocks rose to meet me
Tall rocks, short rocks
sharp rocks, round rocks:
some with the staid steps
of war-wise warriors
others with the gaysome gaits
of pandering pilgrims.

The rocks rose to meet me
eloquent in their deafening silence.
The rocks rose
their shadows a robe
of ungatherable hems

IV
(*The drums quieting*)

I saw the invisible toe-marks
of Èṣìdálè
indelible on the spine-less column
of rocks
unrubbable like a birthmark
older than God
hieroglyphed when earth was molten pap

sculpted into stone by the busy hands
of wind and water.

I saw toe-marks
which laked the rain
for the waiting sun
thirsty like a Sahara camel
I read the cipher tattooed
on the biceps of stone
open like a book of oracles.

The rocks rose to meet me
their legs lithesome with lithic lore.
At every step the earth shook
like an ancient deck
trees trembled from roof to root.
The rocks rose to meet me
with ankle-bells of ploding pods
and seed scattered like a million beads.
The rocks rose to meet my wanderer eyes
singing songs of sunken suns and worsted winds:

   with such defiant brows
   with such unfurrowed faces

just what have the rains been doing?

1. *Oroole*. A pyramid-shaped rock, also in Ikere.
2. *Amoye*. Amoye Grammar School, sited under the shadows of *Oroole*.

HARVESTCALL

I
(*To be chanted to lively bata music*)

This is Iyanfowọrọgi
where, garnished in green
pounded yam rested its feted arms
on the back of stooping stakes.
This is Iyanfọwọrọgi
where valiant heaps cracked, finally,
from the unquenchable zeal of fattening yams.

This is Iyanfoworogi
where yams, ripe and randy,
waged a noisy war against the knife;
here where, subdued by fire,
efùrù[1] provoked mouthful clamor
from the combat of hungry wood:
    the pestle fights the mortar
    the mortar fights the pestle
    a dough of contention smoothes down
    the rugged anger of hunger

Here where yam wore the crown
in the reign of swollen roots
amid a retinue of vines and royal leaves;
between insistent sky and yielding earth,
the sun mellowed planting pageants
into harvest march,
a fiery pestle in his ripening hand.
this is Iyanfọwọrọgi
where a tempting yam sauntered
out of the selling tray
and the marketplace became a mob
of instant suitors.

210

II

And this Òkè Ènìjù
where coy cobs rocked lustily
in the loin of swaying stalks.
Once here in May
a tasseled joy robed the field
like hemless green.
Once here in May
the sky was a riot of pollen grains
and ivory mills waited (im)patiently
for the browning of gray tassels.

And when June had finally grabbed the year
by her narrow waist
Corncobs flashed their milky teeth
in disrobing kitchens.
Plenty's season announced its coming
and the humming mill at dawn
suddenly became the village heart.

III

(Finally) Ògbèsè Odò
where cotton pods, lips duly parted
by December's sun,
draped busy farmsteads
in a harvest of smiles.
Here a blooming loom curtailed
the tiger claws of the harmattan
and earth's wardrobe lent a garb
to every season.

IV
(Music lowers in tempo, becoming solemn)

But where are they?

Where are they gone:
aróso, fèrègèdè, òtíílí, pàkala[1]
which beckoned lustily to the reaping basket

Where are they
the yam pyramids which challenged the sun
in busy barns
Where are they
the pumpkins which caressed earthbreast
like mammary burdens
Where are they
the pods which sweetened harvest air
with the clatter of dispersing seeds?
Where are they? Where are they gone?

Uncountable seeds lie sleeping
in the womb of earth
uncountable seeds
awaiting the quickening tap
of our waking finger.
With our earth so warm
How can our hearth be so cold?

1. *Aróso, fèrègèdè, òtíílí, pàkala.* All four types of peas.

LET EARTH'S PAIN BE SOOTHED

(for the one who brought rainy news from Under-the-Rock)

(to the accompaniment of a flute and/or the rain drum)

The sky carries a boil of anguish
Let it burst

Our earth has never lingered so dry
in the season of falling showers
clouds journey over trees and over hills
miserly with their liquid treasure

The sky carries a boil of anguish
Let it burst

Prostrate like famished horses
brown hills cast vacant looks
at balded plains where playing kids
provoke the dust in what once was
the cradle of green

The sky carries a boil of anguish
Let it bursts

Dust
dust in brewing kitchens
dust in eating halls
dust in busy bedrooms
dust in scheming boardrooms
dust in retrenching factories
dust in power brothels

The sky carries a boil of anguish
Let it burst

Let it rain today
    that parched throats may sing
Let it rain

    that earth may heal her silence
Let it rain today
    that cornleaves may clothe the hills
Let it rain
    that roots may swell the womb of lying plains
Let it rain today
    that stomachs may shun the rumble of thunder
Let it rain
    that children may bath and bawl and brawl

The sky carries a boil of anguish
Let it burst

The roofs have been silent too long
the seeds noiseless in the dormitory of the soil
the earth has been lying too long, and songless.

Time to leap, time to lilt

Let the sky's boil of anguish burst today
The pain of earth be soothed.

FIRST RAIN

a tingling tang awakes the nose
when the first rain has just clipped
the wing of the haughty dust
a cooling warmth embraces
our searching soles
as the land vapor rises
like a bootless infantry

and
through her liberated pores
 our earth breathes again.

RAINDRUM

The roofs sizzle at the waking touch,
talkative like kettledrums
tightened by the iron fingers of drought

Streets break into liquid dance
gathering legs in the orchestra of the road
Streets break into liquid dance
gliding eloquently down the apron of the sky

A stray drop saunters down the thatch
of my remembrance
waking memories long dormant
under the dry leaves of time:

    of caked riverbeds
    and browned pastures
    of baking noons
    and grilling nights
    of earless cornfields
    and tired tubers

Then
Lightning strikes its match of rain
Barefoot, we tread the throbbing earth.

Renewed

MEET ME AT OKERUKU

Meet me at Okeruku[1]
where earth is one compact
of reddening powder
daubed coquettishly
on the harmattan brow
of trembling houses

And when the rains are here
when this dust is clod and clay
show me your camwood shoes
show me hurried toemarks
on the ciphered pages of narrow alleys
awaiting the liquid eraser
of the next shower

1. *Okeruku.* A red-earth district in Ikere.

BUT SOMETIMES WHEN IT RAINS

But sometimes when it rains
and an angry thunder raps earth's ears
with its hands of fire
Sometimes when it rains
and a heartless storm beheads
the poor man's house
like some long-convicted felon.

    Sometimes when it rains
    you wonder who sent the skies weeping

Sometimes when it rains
and an impregnable mahogany falls
across your farmward path
sometimes when it rains
and a streamlet swollen with watery pride
drowns your fields and tender tubers

    Sometimes when it rains
    you wonder who sent the skies weeping

Sometimes when it rains
and a diligent tryst is washed out
by a careless downpour
sometimes when it rains
and a callous mist thickens
between you and the waiting one
sometimes when it rains
dreams are wet with the desperate longing
of a jilted embrace

You wonder who sent the skies weeping
sometimes when it rains.

FARMER-BORN

Farmer-born peasant-bred
I have frolicked from furrow to furrow
sounded kicking tubers in the womb
of quickening earth
and fondled the melon breasts
of succulent ridges.

Farmer-born peasant-bred
I have traced the earthworm's intricate paths
on the map of dawn
heeded dew-call to the upland farm
and, sun-sent, have sought *iroko*[1] refuge
at hungry noons.

Farmer-born peasant-bred
I have lived on the aroma
of fresh-felled forests
relished the delicious symmetry
of *akee apple*[2] colors
and plucked the pendulous promise of ripening pawpaw

Farmer-born peasant-bred
I have rattled the fleshy umbrella
of mushroom jungles
rustled the compost carpet of fallen leaves
and savored the songful clatter
of opening pods

Farmer-born peasant-bred
classroom-bled
I have thrown open my kitchen doors

1. *Iroko.* Large tree found in the rainforest; also called "the African oak."
2. *akee apple.* Tropical fruit with a pink bell-shaped pod (green when
   unripe), cream-white flesh, and glossy black seeds.

and asked hunger to take a seat,
my stomach a howling dump
for Carolina rice.

OURS TO PLOUGH, NOT TO PLUNDER

The earth is ours to plough and plant
the hoe is her barber
the dibble her dimple

Out with mattocks and machetes
bring calabash trays and rocking baskets
let the sweat which swells earth root
relieve heavy heaps of their tuberous burdens

Let wheatfields raise their breadsome hands
to the ripening sun
let legumes clothe the naked bosom
of shivering mounds
let the pawpaw swell and swing
its headward breasts

Let water spring
from earth's unfathomed fountain
let gold rush
from her deep unseeable mines
hitch up a ladder to the dodging sky
let's put a sun in every night

Our earth is an unopened grainhouse,
a bustling barn in some far, uncharted jungle
a distant gem in a rough unhappy dust
This earth is
    ours to work not to waste
    ours to man not to maim
This earth is ours to plough, not to plunder

OUR EARTH WILL NOT DIE
(To a solemn, almost elegiac tune)

Lynched
  the lakes
Slaughtered
  the seas
Mauled
  the mountains

But our earth will not die

  Here
    there
      everywhere

a lake is killed by the arsenic urine
from the bladder of profit factories
a poisoned stream staggers down the hills
coughing chaos in the sickly sea
the wailing whale, belly up like a frying fish,
crests the chilling swansong of parting waters.

But our earth will not die.

  Who lynched the lakes. Who?
  Who slaughtered the seas. Who?
  Whoever mauled the mountains. Whoever?

Our earth will not die

  And the rain
  the rain falls, acid, on balding forests
  their branches amputated by the septic daggers
  of tainted clouds

Weeping willows drip mercury tears
in the eye of sobbing terrains
a nuclear sun rises like a funeral ball
reducing man and meadow to dust and dirt.

But our earth will not die.

Fishes have died in the waters.   Fishes.
Birds have died in the trees.   Birds.
Rabbits have died in their burrows.   Rabbits.

But our earth will not die

(Music turns festive, louder)

Our earth will see again
eyes washed by a new rain
the westering sun will rise again
resplendent like a new coin.
The wind, unwound, will play its tune
trees twittering, grasses dancing;
hillsides will rock with blooming harvests
the plains batting their eyes of grass and grace.
The sea will drink its heart's content
when a jubilant thunder flings open the skygate
and a new rain tumbles down
in drums of joy.
Our earth will see again

this earth, OUR EARTH.

From
A Nib
in the Pond

THE WORD

is a pod
quick with unspoken seeds
exploding in the dry season
of occasion

is an egg
broken,
it spreads
ungatherably

ear's food
mind's nurture
router of silences
sun of noons of action

CALLING A SPADE

No need hiding
in the tabernacle of words
so easily swept off
by the storm of anger

No need camouflaging
behind a flimsy jungle
of occult id-ioms
the metaphor of protest
flips every leaf
in the book of change

Spade callers they are
who till the fertilest terrains
for the richest harvests
knowing as they do that

the simple word
is the shortest distance
between two minds

There is no pet name for
injustice
Poverty
    has no bank for nicknames.

THE POET

is not gadfly
stinging putrefying carcasses
a
lone
in garbage lanes
no closet ink
can wash soiled streets
without the detergent
of collective action

is not a maverick
self-
consciously
deaf
to the homing whistle
through frayed jeans
can be seen, threadbare,
the flimsy texture
of feigning rebels

is not a prophet,
God's hollow ventriloquist,
auguring past futures
in dated tongues
the poet's eyes are washed
in the common spring
though seeing beyond
the hazy horizon
of lowering skies

The poet's pen is
the cactus by the stream
(shorn of its forbidding thorns)
each stem a nib

towards the field of action
its sap the ink of succor
when doubt's drought
assaults the well

Who says the poet
should leave the muck
unraked?
in a land of choking mud
how can the poet
strut
clean
in feathered sandals
and
pretend to the world
he never smells?

SHAPING CLAY

Make me your clay
and shape me
shape me to your heart's content
baby me in your molding palms
their lines birthmarks
on my supple back
and when your potter's will is done
wean me off to your emboldening kiln

Make me your seed
and plant me
plant me in the lush valley
of your loamy bosom
and on the fifth day
watch my bladesome sprout
cut through the dewy shyness of earth
watch me tame stubborn weeds
watch me bloom your barn
with bounteous harvests

Make me your song
and sing me
sing me clean and clear
like a whistle
mind my matter, mould my manner
for what is the song
without the singing
the singing
without the song?

Sing me
in temples and taverns
in bedchambers and marketplaces
in farmlands and factory floors

in GRAs[1] and sprawling slums

Shape me
Plant me
Sing me

To wake a slumbering world.

.

1. GRAs. Government Reserved Areas (exclusive, privileged)

LIKE THE BEE
(after Francis Bacon)

Not like the spider
draping crowded rooms
in the wanton web
of flimsy looms
a welter of legs spinning
silky bridges, fragile,
for the empty feet of air

Not like the wood-insect
carpentering logs to fashion
its own prison
stockaded pupae peeping
behind bars of enslaving labor

But like the bee
brewing one honey
from the nectars
of several seasons
pleasing the bud
of every clime.

NOT STANDING STILL

I grew weary of the tyranny of water
and spat in the sea
I grew wary of the power of the sun
and lit candles at noon

A juicy rodent ran across
my morning path
I aimed my water-pot
at its teasing head

the quarry mocked
the potsherds of my lust
but it didn't go
without a dripping tail

Not standing still
is the beginning of battle
he will never pluck the fruit
whose back caresses the earth

The circle which has a beginning
also has an end
a little patience is what it needs
the stammerer will call

his father's name.

A NIB IN THE POND

We read your lines
opening up the earth
like a book of paths
hear your voice
melting the wax of a thousand seasons

You who throw a nib
in the pond of silence
the ripples in your inkpot
convulse barracks and power brothels
overturning plots of plunder
lying on calculating tables
like poison bowls

We sing the lines
and hear our voice
read the words
and see ourselves
in the mirror of every letter

Now
though hands are two
we know which wipes the anus
there is a fork in the road
but we know the shorter way home.

SCRIBBLING HOE

The farmer
pens the pages of earth
with the nib
of a forge-fresh hoe
scribbles mounds
between margins of blooming corn
cursives paragraphs of legumes
in ruled furrows
his barn is a library
of nourishing seasons

QUESTIONS FOR A PANDERING POET

What is the poet doing
in the corridors of power:

romping to the ravaging rumblings
of constipated stomachs

nodding to the killsome lies
of reptiles of state

swaying to the rustling silk
of state fops

festering on the sputumed remains
of political tables

clapping for the airy ramblings
of ghosted tirades

peeping at the eunuch beds
of noisy chambers

licking the bloodied boots
of goose steppers?

Of man and mammon
duty and diadem
nous and nescience
who still argues
which side the poet should be?

ÀTẸ̀WỌ́LARÁ[1]

(for Tunde Odunlade)

We have teemed in desert temples
crawled in mystery mosques
mumbling carrion of forgotten tongues

We have swarmed shrinking shrines
of skeletal gods
and altars weighted down
by termites of faith

Reared as we are
to take life
as a knotty theorem
of unarguable givens

And cry the people:
Who shall save us?

Who shall save us
from a sea red with death's threat
and the armed legion
of mercedesed Pharaohs?

Then
came a whisper
urgent like harmattan finger
prompting like a prick:

wake you up
and befriend your mind
you will see the answers
permanenced in the lines
of your palm

1. *Àtẹ̀wọ́lará.* The hand is the best companion.

LETTER FROM THE PUBLISHER

Please find herewith
your manuscript returned
sorry we do not publish
unknown writers.

FOR JOHN DONNE

Hopping from bed to bed
like a bug irrepressibly on heat
your roving songs crumpled a thousand sheets
parting trilling lips in seminal closets

Loving, your love songs
penetrating like a barbed baton
conceived *new founde lands* and Americas
solemnized marriages in bug bellies

Every metaphor sweats
from the orgasmic gasps
of fallopian journeys

Then
your compass legs (now trousered)
completed the circle
womansong mellowed into godsong
the altar jilted the bed

Jack to John, Donne to Dean
Don Juan to John Donne

O metaphor of merry metamorphosis!

PROMISE LAND

Should we should we not pray
for them who thunder promises
from prefab podiums
feeding famished ears with vows
of promised lands

Should we should we not pray
for them who banish thought
from action
murder reason, exile hope
hang poets for their dreams
claiming every right to think
without a mind

Should we should we not pray
by their bedside
who ravish our future
in castles sentried
by brass buttons and eunuch cannon

Should we should we not pray
for them who scorch our sun
machete our moon
ordering us to greet
with bugles and drums
the majesty of their power

?   ?   ?   ?

Arise
you for so long crushed
under the elephant's weight

We shall reach the promised land
through the wilderness of our palm.

COLLAGE

Only one brief night
and a bride becomes a wife

*

Fancying millionaires
without trampled scruples
is like imagining omelettes
without shattered shells

*

Comrades or come-raids
trail-blazers or blaze-trailers
damask or the mask

*

For every finger you point
three others are arrows
towards your heart

*

Hail liberals
who give with the left
and take with the right

*

Be a good citizen:
don't argue

*

From praying ground to preying ground
from democracy to demoncrazy

from conscience to con-science

*

Waste time
and a wound becomes a sore

*

We demand justice
they give us judgment

*

If you turn the world
into a lake of poison
you will drink a bowl

*

Allies or all lies
adultery or adult tree
message or mess age

*

Heathrow finger in immigrant panties
Virginity test in a fair free isle

*

When the pestle fights the mortar
It is the yam that suffers

*

The sky
Is our village umbrella:
If you tear the portion
Above your roof,

There will be rain-water
In my inner rooms

*

All that glitters
Has to be gold

*

One two three four
Let's end the Arms Race
Not end the Human Race

*

Curse me
with a gentle eye
Damn me
with a nod
Sting me
with a stunning smile

*

After you
there will be no blank pages
in my book of memory

*

Nuclear clouds
have no silver lining

I AM THE COMMON MAN

I
am the sturdiest plank
in a campaign platform
stamped countless times
to pound lies into a dough of deceit.

I
am the base element
in the chemistry of numbers
added
subtracted
multiplied
at will
in the politics of fractions

I
am a housing problem
depression agent
for whom the Vagrancy Act
was lobbied into being

I
who put the foam
in the soapbox
fire in the thunder
of close-fisted harangues

I
am the toast
in every palace
the dessert
of royal belches

But
I am truly
the flower of the forest
the salt of the sea

the sun of the sky
the wheel of a moving world

Unfellable
like a tree with a million roots
I will shake the earth
with giant fruits
lading the four winds
with seeds of change.

NOON YET
(for Femi Ogunmola)

I didn't pluck my flowers
too early in the forest
so they do not droop
with lengthening shadows

I didn't cook my yam
in the pot of night
so its flavor doesn't perish
before the waking mouth

I will not shout out myself
before the festival of songs
so a frog of excess
doesn't jump into my eager throat

He who listens well
will hear the footsteps of ants
he who probes the bloom
will hear fragrances of vanished gardens

If I live long enough
I will eat meat
the size of a thousand elephants
my teeth all ivory, my dusk a golden feast

Time it may take
time it may take
the raw yam will turn
a smiling morsel

Time it may take
the stammerer will
one day pronounce
his father's name

248

From
Songs of the
Marketplace

POETRY IS

not the esoteric whisper
of an excluding tongue
not a clap trap
for a wondering audience
not a learned quiz
entombed in Grecoroman lore

Poetry is
a lifespring
which gathers timbre
the more throats it plucks
harbinger of action
the more minds it stirs

Poetry is
the hawker's ditty
the eloquence of the gong
the lyric of the marketplace
the luminous ray
on the grass's morning dew

Poetry is
what the soft wind
musics to the dancing leaf

what the sole tells the dusty path
what the bee hums to the alluring nectar
what rainfall croons to the lowering eaves

Poetry is
no oracle's kernel
for a sole philosopher's stone

Poetry
is
man
meaning
to man.

251

SIREN
(Music of the Visiting Power)

Siren Siren Siren
Police acrobats on motorbikes
wielding whips with consummate dispatch
the road must be cleared at once
for which worthy ruler
ever shares the right of way?

Siren Siren Siren
the clangorous convoy
of powers and power brokers
conditional in Mercedes back
far, very far, from the maddening crowd

Siren Siren Siren
kwashiorkored children
waving tattered flags
in the baking sun
(they forfeited the day's meal
to cheer their Excellencies)
orchestrated cultural dancers
dripping drums of sweat
in raffia shrouds
partymen kangarooing
to keep the crowd in place

Siren Siren Siren
Even on highways where potholes
snail the jaguar
they manage not to see
a land debowelled by erosion
cornfields withering
and yam tendrils yellowing
on tubers smaller than a palm kernel

blind are they
to the seeds of tomorrow's famine

Siren Siren Siren
and bunting and banners
and brazen bombasts
their Excellence love
the sound of words

Siren Siren Siren
no time for dry days
and dark nights
or food whose price
costs a ton of gold
no time for hospitals
and schools and roads
their Excellencies are not here
for the begging bickerings
of a faceless rural crowd

Siren siren siren
and the air heavy
with love of state
organized grins
made up cheers
rehearsed pledges

But babies contorted
in mother's backs
are question marks
for tomorrow's answer.

THE NIGERIAN RAILWAY

dark sna
ky str
uctures
      tor   tuous
milli
      pede on
legs
      of   iron
crawl   ing
wear   ily

fromswamptosavannah.

ON SEEING A BENIN MASK
IN A BRITISH MUSEUM
(for FESTAC 77)

Here stilted on plastic
A god deshrined
Uprooted from your past
Distanced from your present
Profaned sojourner in a strange land

Rescued from a smoldering shrine
By a victorianizing expedition
Traded in for an O.B.E.
Across the shores

Here you stand, chilly,
Away from your clothes
Gazed at by curious tourists savoring
Parallel lines on your forehead
Parabola on your cheek
Semicircles of your eyebrows
And the solid geometry of your lips
Here you stand
Dissected by alien eyes.

Only what becomes is becoming
A noose does not become a chicken's neck
Who ever saw a deity dancing *langbalangba*[1]
To the carious laugh of philistine revelers?

    Ìyá jàjèjì Égbè
    Ilé ẹni lèṣọ́ yẹ ni[2]

Retain the tight dignity of those lips
Unspoken grief becomes a god

When all around are alien ears
Unable to crack the kernel of the riddle.

1. langbalangba: undifignifingly; gracelessly
2. Suffering afflicts the stranger in an alien land.
   One is most valued in one's own home.

MINDSCOPE
(for B.J.)

"Thou shalt not," they say
"Why not?!," I ask

and instantly turning
an eddy of questions
my mind probes belief's underbelly
pulps tradition's iron curtain
into paper screen unriddled
with the nib of search

WHY
unevils a cyclorama of seeing
deep expanse of knowing
across a radiant universe of vision

mindscoping truths contrabanded
by dogma, embargoed by mystery's
customs, uniformed guards of nescience

and rays fall back
enlightening doubts,
radiating marvels,
leveling mountains.

to each eye, light
to each mind, question
to each conscience, will
to each will, action.